Survival Fish Harvesting

Harvesting Fish for Survival Protein in Wilderness or SHTF Situations in the Easiest and Most Effective Ways Possible

PAUL STEVENS

ISBN: 978-0-9869583-2-8

DEDICATION

I would like to dedicate this book to my wife Lynn, my two adult children Shannon and Trevor, to Lynn's two adult children Nathan and Kate, and to our grandchild Hudson. Family is the best reason to learn and practice preparedness, and family truly is the number one reason to strive for survival in a chaotic world.

TABLE OF CONTENTS

PAUL STEVENS

WARNING

Methods and techniques described in this book for catching fish may be illegal in your area and you are advised to check with local game, conservation, or sport authorities before trying any of them.

Descriptions of early or current preservation techniques are taken from reputable sources, but the author or publisher makes no claim to special expertise or knowledge in this area. You are advised to study the source material and seek the opinion of experts.

ACKNOWLEDGMENTS

For my love of the outdoors and the appreciation of the myriad ways it can provide for us I have to thank my parents, Mary and Doug Stevens. Both lived through the depression and had that experience behind them. They both also lived close to the land, spending many hours of their youth working in gardens, playing in the meadows and forested bush that they lived close to and, in the case of my mother, helping the family to procure a living on not always friendly farm acreage.

I would like to mention my Uncle Bill, Mom's brother, who shared her early life on the farm, but also engaged in trapping, hunting and the regular ingenious fabrication that is part of the problem-solving farm lifestyle. Uncle Bill with his wife Olga also intensively farmed their half acre lot, raised chinchillas, built their own greenhouse and shared his love of reading and learning with his own family and mine.

The genesis of this book was an episode I listened to of Jack Spirko's "The Survival Podcast." Jack started TSP in 2008, recording shows on his daily hour long commute to his daytime work. Jack recorded a podcast about how fish could be a tremendous source of protein in good times and bad. In truly bad times, fish may be easier to acquire than other animal sources. Listening to that episode got me thinking and I came up with the idea of developing a book that looked at all possible ways of harvesting them.

I would like to thank my wife Lynn, for putting up with my passions and strange interests and her faithful support.

I would like to extend my thanks the Cheryl Harrison for generously taking the time to provide a thorough reading of the manuscript and for her excellent suggestions for changes to improve readability.

And a sincere thank you to Jason Houle and Nabe Nery for technical advice and suggestions after reading an early copy of the book..

Paul Stevens.

1 INTRODUCTION

A dependable source of food is essential to health and optimum functioning of your body. We've all heard you can survive for 2 weeks (or more) without eating, but your strength, and mental sharpness starts decreasing pretty rapidly after a few days. The brain uses about 20% of your body's energy. In a survival situation, the brain is probably your most important resource. Having your brain dumbing down just as you are faced with making more and tougher decisions about the situations you face is not a recipe for success.

While it isn't difficult to store carbohydrates (rice, dried beans, wheat), protein isn't as easy or inexpensive. When you are feasting on good protein sources, your brain has access to the raw materials it needs to produce neurotransmitters like serotonin and dopamine. These two amino acids are important to keep up our energy levels, mental clarity, mood, and our ability to remain calm and collected when faced with stress.

FISH AS A PROTEIN SOURCE

There are few sources of protein better than fish. It is typically low in fat, and in the fattier cold water varieties like salmon, the fat is of the healthy omega-3 variety. On average a sedentary male will need 56 g/day of protein, and a sedentary female will need 46 grams of protein a day.

Fish can vary in protein content from 62 g/100g for cod to 15 /100g for catfish. Common freshwater varieties like bass, perch and trout come in between 22 and 25g/100g. A large man, engaged in hard physical labour will need around 120g of protein a day. In a survival situation, your needs will likely lie somewhere between sedentary and hard physical labour so, for that large man, we can estimate 80 – 90g of protein or almost a pound of bass.

Of course, if you are fortunate enough to have some oatmeal and powdered milk for breakfast, and some rice and beans as a side dish with your fish, your daily needs from fish will go down.

fig 2

The important message here is that, if you can figure out how to harvest some fish, you can greatly supplement your existing supplies of protein.

Anyone who has ever spent hours in a boat, or on the side of a riverbank, sitting and waiting for the fish to strike, will not be much encouraged with the thought of using fish as a food source.

fig 3

If that's you, then you may be approaching this possible solution with a certain amount of doubt. Just think of this; wherever you are, you probably live in a jurisdiction that has strict rules about how and when you can catch fish. Those rules make it tough to succeed in fishing.

There are hard and fast rules, with strict penalties for non-compliance (like the ability to seize your boat, motor and the vehicle that transported you to your fishing location), to ensure you follow those rules. They wouldn't need all of those rules if it was very hard to catch fish.

These restrictions apply to rod fishing. Most jurisdictions do not allow traps, non-commercial nets, and for most species, no set lines or spearfishing. Are you getting a sense of where I am going? In a survival situation, or a breakdown in society, fish may provide a relatively easy, ready source of food, if you can get past the simple rod/hook/bait or lure paradigm.

Note: There are some species that have few if any restrictions. For instance, where I live in Ontario, there is no season on perch, sunfish and crappies. Limits vary from 15 to 30 fish on a conservation license. Carp, bowfin, and sucker can be taken with a spear or bow during certain seasons, and have no limits. Smelt (no limit) and Lake Whitefish (same as angling limits) may be taken with a dip net.

I found a 2011 article published by the Inland Fisheries Institute in Poland, about fish poaching in the Ukraine. The article noted "Poaching usually originate from a lack of alternative food resources or sources of income for local communities and more often occurs in developing countries." In other words, it is a survival activity.

More to the point, the article listed the types and number of illegal methods used, so is a good guide to what works best, at least as far as the poachers are concerned. Gill nets were the most popular piece of equipment, with 47 occurrences. Next came lift nets, which they found in use 18 times, seine nets which were used in 18 offences, electrofishing (usually with homemade devices) was found 9 times, spearfishing was the method of choice 7 times and concussion (striking large rocks sticking out of the water with sledge hammers to create an underwater shockwave to stun the fish) was used by 6 offenders.

I cover all of these methods and more in this book. At the risk of repeating myself I will once again state that what we are going to look at in this volume is survival fishing, which is a very different story than sport fishing.

WARNING: Much of what I will be talking about in this book is illegal in much of the world. You need to understand the laws in your own area. However, laws may not apply to your situation if you are forced into considering these methods. For example, if you are in a true survival situation in the wilderness, no court will prosecute you for using these methods. In a true societal breakdown, authorities will have more important considerations to deal with than how you might be acquiring your daily supper or lunch.

SAFETY CONSIDERATIONS

Safety first, so here are a few simple cautions about eating fish, whether caught by you, or found in or near a water source.

Don't eat fish with:

1. Unpleasant odour

2. Pale, slimy gills

3. Sunken eyes

4. Flabby skin

5. Flesh which remains dented when pressed

6. On the ocean shore, avoid all crustaceans above the high water mark

7. On the ocean shore , avoid all aquatic life during a red tide

8. Avoid cone shaped shells

Eating spoiled or rotten fish may cause diarrhea, nausea, cramps, vomiting, itching, paralysis, or a metallic taste in the mouth. These symptoms appear suddenly, one to six hours after eating. Induce vomiting if symptoms appear.

2 CATCHING FISH

ANGLING

I know the bulk of this book is about unconventional methods of taking fish, but I would be remiss if I didn't quickly cover straight up angling first. If you are someone who is concerned with outdoor survival, you may already have thought about fish as a food source. Maybe you pack a length of fishing line and a selection of hooks with you, whenever you are hitting the boonies. If you are a prepper, maybe this is a food source that has slipped by you. In either case, pay attention to what comes next. I am betting that there are going to be some ideas here that you haven't considered.

If you are in a situation where you have the option of having a fishing rod, then you should have one. There are numerous telescoping solutions available, if space or packing is a consideration. I am not going to make specific recommendations because the perfect solution for you depends on your financial resources and your circumstance: backpacker, off roader, wild river runner, or home prepper considering additions to your existing storage. Needless to say, in any case, you shouldn't be relying on one solution.

If you are filling in your home preps then you have some additional space, so make sure you have a couple of sets of fishing gear available. If you are packing, make sure you have your emergency fishing kit along for the ride, and not packed in the same location as your conventional rod and reel.

fig 4

I live in a rural area, and regularly go to a local auction house. Fishing equipment appears at every third or fourth auction and great selections on used items are available at 25% retail or less. You can also find fishing equipment at yard sales, thrift stores and estate sales. There is no excuse not to be as fully equipped as you want to be.

For a survival situation go with a higher test line. What fish are likely to be in the body of water you might be harvesting from? After reading some of the harvesting suggestions in this book, think about what your requirements might be considering your local environment. There's a world of difference between a large yellow perch and a large carp or catfish. Don't select a line weight that will leave you wishing you had packed something a little stronger. It makes sense to have a couple of different weight lines available.

Fluorocarbon lines are virtually invisible underwater. They are more expensive, but let's face it; we aren't talking about running through hundreds of yards of this stuff. A bonus with fluorocarbon line is it's abrasion resistance, as compared to monofilament. Braided line has a much higher strength to diameter ratio than either monofilament or fluorocarbon, but it isn't very stretchy. This can make a difference. A fish can shake the hook off after striking. I am not going to go into a deep discussion on the merits or disadvantages of the three different lines, since I am not an expert at sport fishing. There is lots of information available both online and in your local library or at the magazine stand. The only thing I will add is that you want to consider what your primary target species will be. If you are targeting pan fish then fluorocarbon or monofilament might be the way to go. If you are considering catfish, maybe you want to use braided. The best advice is to get a feel for all three types of line by fishing yourself locally. Then make your choice.

You will need a selection of hooks. Use the appropriate size. As I said above with regards to line, you need to know what you are fishing for. You could be in a situation where you can haul in a mess of 6" sunfish, taking small pieces of worm, on a # 4 hook at the rate of one every couple of minutes. You wouldn't likely catch any of them on a 4/0 hook.

Think about your situation, do some research on what bodies of water you will have access to in the scenario you are planning for, and make some choices. You will probably want to expand your selection, considering the cost of hooks, and the little space they take up.

Later in the book I talk about trot lines, setlines, drop lines and snagging. All of these methods depend on multiple hooks and/or lines. You would not be remiss to pack away 100 – 150 hooks to fully make effective use of these methods, considering that in just a few hours you could easily put out 10 lines with 10 – 15 hooks each. This doesn't even allow for replacement of missing, or broken hooks as you go about harvesting fish.

Trotline catfish fishermen typically use circle hooks. Circle hooks show in studies that they are better at holding onto hooked fish. They also tend to snag on debris at a lower rate than J-style hooks.

Additional handy to have equipment would be a selection of treble hooks, swivels, sinkers a bobber or two and maybe a few guide rings for whatever rod you have. I'll talk a little more about nets later on.

If you are in almost any community setting, either urban or rural, you can put together some kind of fishing kit. But what if you are out in the wilderness someplace, with no buildings, houses or dollar stores nearby? No problem! You can make your own fishhooks, nets and traps and also use several other methods to obtain fish in a survival situation.

3 EXPEDIENT FISHING

WILDENESS SURVIAL FISHING KIT

In this chapter I talk about "expedient fishing." That is, what do you do if you are out someplace with no gear. Of course, that should never happen. If you are going to be someplace where it is plausible you could be stranded or in a situation where you must find your own sources of food for multiple days, you absolutely should have a fishing kit with you. So I have assembled what is a reasonable kit, that can be used to put some of the strategies discussed in this book into practice.

This is a lightweight kit, that you might take with you hiking, camping or have packed into your off-road vehicle. Some of this stuff you should have with you as part of your regular survival gear.

- Minimum of 15 metres/50 feet of paracord – for use with set lines, trot lines, drop lines, jug lines etc. Also can be used as cord for expedient nets.
- Fluorocarbon fishing line 6-10 pound test, 100 yard spool
- A pack of 100 hooks in assorted sizes like #4, #1, 1/0,and 2/0 or whatever is appropriate for your situation
- A pack of treble hooks in 3/0 or 4/0
- A pack of 20-50 snap or barrel swivels
- A pack of 15 – 20 sinkers, various weights
- A pack of 50 – 100 assorted split-shot
- A lightweight, but powerful flashlight
- Spear/harpoon/gigging head, purchased or easily homemade

Depending on the space and weight considerations you might want to include a replacement mesh for a landing net. By using a flexible bough, you can quickly create an expedient landing net that can also be used as a dip net for small fish or crayfish.

In this book I talk about snagging as a method of fish harvesting, hence the treble hooks. If you are snagging carp, you might want multiple 5/0 or larger treble hooks.

If you have the space, consider including a spool of braided line, up to 30 pounds. Braided line allows you to cast further, and the lack of stretch means you can feel a fish on the line more easily, with extra line out.

The flashlight can be used for night fishing with a spear or snagging line.

If you are familiar with the "survival fishing kit in a pill bottle" suggestions from some sources, you might be shaking your head. Those mini-kits are assembled on the premise (assuming the suggested components have any premise behind them) that you will be going after pan fish or small fish up to 8" in size, since they tend to be easier to catch on crude equipment. You are expected to catch them one at a time. You are not expected to have to feed more than yourself.

The equipment I suggest in the above kit will allow you to easily and quickly create 10 to 15 fishing set ups that can be used in a "set and forget mode," allowing you to potentially harvest half a dozen or more fish a couple of times a day, assuming there are fish available. These setups can be left to work passively during the day or overnight while you go to work on other aspects of survival, like starting a fire, finding fuel, creating a shelter, laying out signal material, assisting injured etc.

HAND GATHERING

The sea side tends to be a food rich location, which is one of the reasons it was settled early by humans. Seafood can be found in coastal zones as well as coastal rivers around the world. Seafood suitable for gathering by hand includes aquatic invertebrates such as molluscs and crustaceans, as well as aquatic plants.

Shellfish can be collected from intertidal areas using a spade or rake. Some molluscs commonly gathered are oysters, clams, scallops and cockles. Some crustaceans commonly gathered are lobster, crayfish, and crabs.

SEAWEEDS

Edible seaweed are algae that can be eaten and used in the preparation of food. They typically contain high amounts of fiber and are a complete protein. They may belong to one of several groups of multicellular algae: the red algae, green algae, or brown algae.

Most edible seaweeds are marine algae whereas most freshwater algae are toxic. Below is a list of, and illustrations of, the most common types of edible seaweed. Research what is available in your area, where it occurs, what time of year is best for harvest and how to best harvest it.

Dulse – *Palmaria palmate*

Dulse grows on the northern coasts of the Atlantic and Pacific Oceans. It is a well-known snack food. It also grows on the shores of Arctic Russia, Arctic Canada, Atlantic Canada, Alaska, Japan, and Korea. In Iceland, where it is known as söl, it has been an important source of dietary fiber throughout the centuries.

 Dulse is a good source of minerals and vitamins compared with other vegetables, contains all trace elements needed by humans, and has a high protein content. It is commonly found from June to September and can be picked by hand when the tide is out. When picked, small snails, shell pieces, and other small particles can be washed or shaken off and the plant then spread to dry. Some gatherers may turn it once and roll it into large bales to be packaged later. It is used as fodder for animals in some countries.

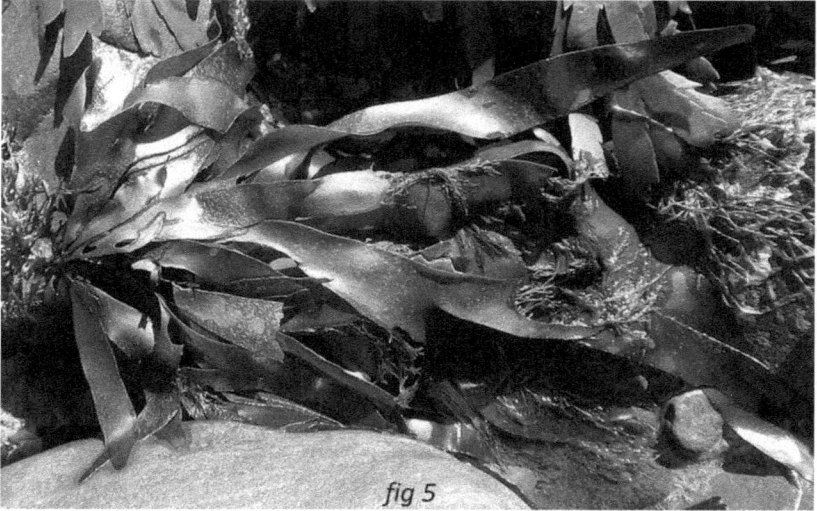

Dulse By Cwmhiraeth - Own work, CC BY-SA 3.0,
https://commons.wikimedia.org/w/index.php?curid=16824956

Fresh dulse can be eaten directly off the rocks before sun-drying. Sun-dried dulse is eaten as is or is ground to flakes or a powder. In Iceland, the tradition is to eat it with butter. It can be pan-fried quickly into chips.

Irish Moss – *Chrondus crispus*

Chondrus crispus—commonly called Irish moss or carrageen moss (Irish carraigín, "little rock")—is a species of red algae which grows abundantly along the rocky parts of the Atlantic coast of Europe and America. It consists of nearly 10% protein and about 15% mineral matter, and is rich in iodine and sulfur. When softened in water it has a sea-like odour and because of the abundant cell wall polysaccharides it will form a jelly when boiled, containing from 20 to 100 times its weight of water.

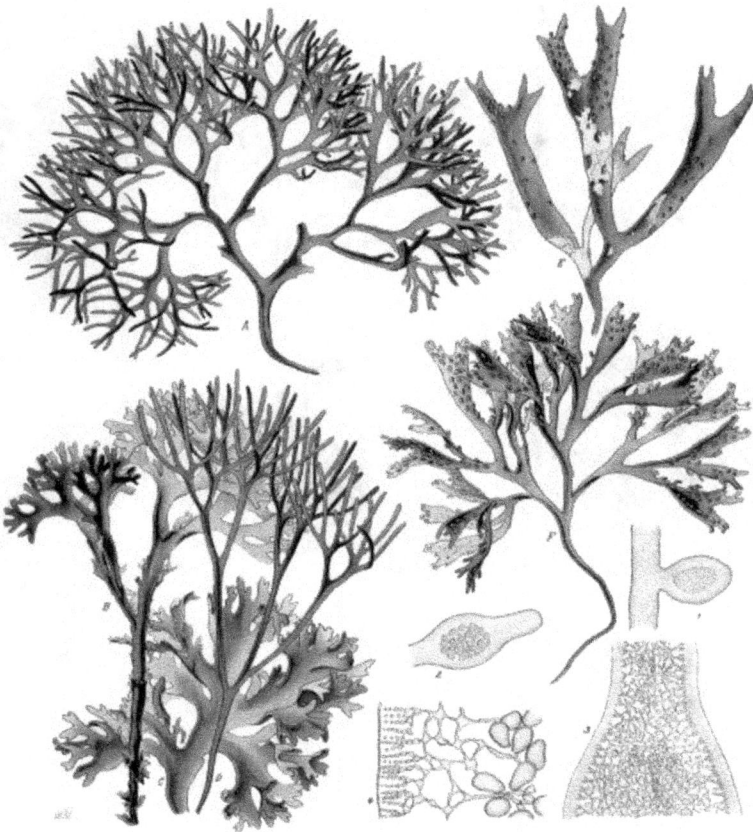

fig 6

Sea Lettuce – *Ulva lactuca*

Ulva lactuca, also known by the common name sea lettuce, is an edible green alga. The distribution is worldwide: Europe, North America (west and east coasts), Central America, Caribbean Islands, South America, Africa, Indian Ocean Islands, South-west Asia, China, Pacific Islands, Australia and New Zealand.

Generally used in soups and salads.

Sea Lettuce By Kristian Peters -- 12 December 2006 -
https://commons.wikimedia.org/w/index.php?curid=1453578

Kelp

Kelp By FASTILY (TALK) https://commons.wikimedia.org/w/index.php?curid=6829518

Kelp is broadly available in the Atlantic as well as the Pacific. While not particularly high in protein or fat, it is rich in minerals and vitamins. Kombu is the type of kelp famously eaten in Japan. Frequently eaten dried it can also be eaten fresh as sashimi.

Wakame

Wakame was likely the most commonly eaten seaweed in Japan, in times past. Wakame was probably a generic term for seaweed in ancient times.

fig 9

Shellfish

The number of edible shellfish is much too long to list here. Just a partial listing of molluscs would include sea snails like abalone, limpets, winkles, conchs and whelks as well as the various clams, mussels, oysters, cockles, scallops, etc.

Many of these can be found between the high water and low water tide mark. Others can be found in depths ranging from 3 feet to 50 feet. Virtually all have been historically harvested by hand using simple implements ranging from knives to rakes.

You need to do research specific to your area for species, time of year for harvest, methods and also current legal limits and dates. Time spent now, will ensure that later, you will be familiar with local target species and methods of collecting.

NOODLING

In parts of the United States, mainly the South, catfish, primarily of the flathead species, is occasionally caught by hand in a technique most often known as noodling. The practitioner is typically looking for flathead catfish, since they live in holes or under brush along rivers and lakes. If you know where to look for them, they are easier to find.

fig 10

Noodler suffers cuts from angry catfish

The noodler places their hand inside the hole, and the catfish moves forward and takes the hand in their mouth in self-defence. Once they are latched on, the noodler lifts them from the water into a boat or onto shore. This is frequently done with a helper, since there is no telling in advance how big the catfish will be.

A typical weight for a noodled catfish is 40 pounds. Noodling can be dangerous, since we are talking water, and a strong, heavy fish fighting for its life. Noodlers often dive in water up to 20 feet deep, while looking for holes. Abandoned catfish holes can be taken over by snapping turtles, alligators, muskrats, snakes and beavers. This is not something I have tried, or am ever likely to try. The next technique though, is something I have done.

TROUT TICKLING

Trout Tickling has probably been used almost as long as humans have tried to catch fish. It is mentioned in Shakespeare's Twelfth Night as a metaphor for bamboozlement. It was a common practice in the UK and used by boys, poachers and working men in times of economic stress, particularly during the 1930s depression-era. Poachers using this method required no nets, rods or lines or any other incriminating equipment if apprehended by the police or gamekeepers.

Thomas Martindale's 1901 book, Sport, Indeed, describes the method used on trout in the River Wear in County Durham:

> *The fish are watched working their way up the shallows and rapids. When they come to the shelter of a ledge or a rock it is their nature to slide under it and rest. The poacher sees the edge of a fin or the moving tail, or maybe he sees neither; instinct, however, tells him a fish ought to be there, so he takes the water very slowly and carefully and stands up near the spot. He then kneels on one knee and passes his hand, turned with fingers up, deftly under the rock until it comes in contact with the fish's tail. Then he begins tickling with his forefinger, gradually running his hand along the fish's belly further and further toward the head until it is under the gills. Then comes a quick grasp, a struggle, and the prize is wrenched out of his natural element, stunned with a blow on the head, and landed in the pocket of the poacher.*

IMPROVISED FISHING GEAR

FISHHOOKS

You can make field-expedient fishhooks from pins, needles, wire, small nails, or almost any small piece of metal, especially if you have your handy multi-tool or some very basic hand tools with you. You can also use wood, bone, coconut shell, thorns, flint, seashell, or tortoise shell. You can also make fishhooks from any combination of these items

A fish hook you make yourself is not going to do the same job as one you have purchased. It will likely be bigger, clumsier, scarier to fish, not as strong, not as sharp and inferior in many other ways. You will also have to spend time making them, so the next time you are in a sporting goods store, a hardware store, or even a dollar store, pick up a pack of assorted sizes and keep them in your pack or vehicle, or your house or garage. Just remember where they are and save yourself some grief. Having said that, let's take a look at improvised hooks that have been used in survival situations or earlier times when hooks were made by hand.

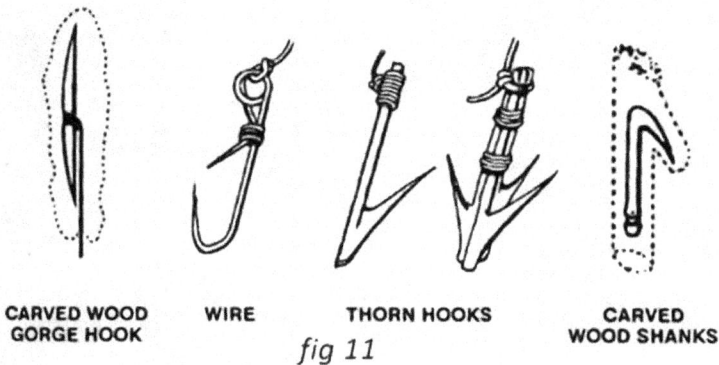

CARVED WOOD GORGE HOOK   WIRE   THORN HOOKS   CARVED WOOD SHANKS

fig 11

In the illustrations above (fig. 11) we can see examples taken from a US military survival manual. Most of these are patterned after hooks made by aboriginal peoples before trade occurred with Europeans.

A gorge is a small shaft of wood, bone, metal, or other material. It is sharp on both ends and notched in the middle where you tie your line. When you pull on the line, one of the points is likely to catch on the side of the fishes gut and the gorge will wind up at right angles to the line, unable to pass back up through the throat.

Below is an improvised lure made by the indigenous people of Tonga, acquired by Captain Cooke on his second or third voyage to the Pacific. (fig. 12)

Image by Oliver James Perkins, Australian Museum

fig 12

IMPROVISED ROD

A rod is extremely useful for survival fishing, even without a reel. It is far simpler to place a baited hook in a specific location if you have a 6' – 8' rod, with a length of line securely tied to the end. You can use a simple flip technique to drop the hook in a back eddy, beside a stone or some other underwater structure. Even if you just want to reach out from the bank a little into deeper water, a rod will ease your way.

If you have access to a source of bamboo great. Because of its superior strength to weight ratio, and its flexibility, bamboo has been a strong choice for fishing rods for centuries. Alternatively a length of sapling, starting about 2.5 cm (1") in diameter and tapering down to 2 cm (3/4") will do nicely. Look for green wood, not dry. A springy action is what you want. The strength of tree species varies so give your potential rod a good bend to make sure it doesn't split easily.

As in all things related to fishing, everything depends on what your target fish is and how you are going to be bringing it in. Brook trout taking a baited hook require a different sort of rod then carp that you are aiming to snag with treble hooks. Use some common sense. The longer the pole, the more awkward it will be to handle, but the more accurately you will be able to place your baited hook.

FISHING LINE

Fishing line has been improvised from any number of sources in the past; everything from boot laces to strands of wool unravelled from a sweater. You can let your imagination run wild. Two of the more handy sources of line are probably the inner strands of paracord, and dental floss. Both are difficult to break and have the advantage of being lighter and narrower than boot laces or the kind of twine you can make in the wilds with different vegetative fibres available to you. The inner strands of paracord are rated for about 17 pounds, quite a respectable number. Paracord is readily available and not expensive. Considering the multiple uses for it, anyone venturing into the boonies should have some in their kit.

Your line should be a couple of feet longer than your pole.

A float will help you detect a bite. Almost anything can be used here; a piece of cork with a slit running lengthwise in it to secure the line, or a bit of foam that your line is knotted around or even a length of stick.

You should have no trouble with sinkers. Your best bet is to make sure you have at least some split shot in your kit. Some cord tightly wrapped around a small stone gives you a weight with ready-made attachment points.

BAIT

There's not much to be said about bait. If you have access to worms, you probably don't need to look any further. If worms are hard to come up with, look for leeches, minnows, frogs, grasshoppers, crickets or maggots.

fig 13

There's not much to be said about bait. If you have access to worms, you probably don't need to look any further. If worms are hard to come up with, look for leeches, minnows, frogs, grasshoppers, crickets or maggots.

You might want to take a look in the gut of the first few fish you manage to catch, to see what or they were taking for their previous meal.

Look at the local environment, the weather and the time of year and you'll come up with dozens of possibilities.

One bait tip I found online was in reference to worms. Someone advised you to put a dab of superglue on your hook and press a (previously wiped dry) worm against the dab. This will keep the worm on the hook even if it gets unhooked after getting hit once or twice. This keeps your hook in business a little longer, increasing your odds of catching lunch. Does your survival kit include a bottle of superglue? It's also pretty useful for holding the edges of minor cuts closed.

4 MULTIPLYING YOUR ANGLING EFFECTIVENESS

MULTIPLE LINES AND HOOKS

The best advice I can give to ensure you catch more fish if you are angling is to have more baited lines in the water for fish to hit. One way to do this is to have multiple rods as in Figure 14.

fig 14

fig. 14a

You can make your own by getting some lengths of PVC pipe of a big enough diameter to drop your rod handle in. Cut them down to 18 – 24" lengths, cut one end on a diagonal, giving you a point, and drive them into the ground on the bank of a river or lake, on a slight angle. If you have multiple rods, drop each one into the PVC's after you have cast your baited hook out. It would be best if you stayed around to check on your lines periodically. Later on we will talk about limb lines, jug lines, and Montagnais nightlines, which are essentially the same principle, but can be left unattended unattended.

SET LINES

There is a pretty wide variance in the definitions of set lines, trot lines, drop lines etc. In this book I am going to describe set lines as a line that either floats, or is fixed at one end.

Why would you use setlines? One way to find an answer would be to ask setline users why THEY use them.

A 2013 thesis written by Benjamin Dickinson did just that when he examined setline fishing in the New River, Virginia. When he asked setliners why they used a setline instead of a rod and reel, 30 of 39 setliners interviewed identified that they could catch more fish by setlining.

Additional answers were that setlines freed up time, by reducing the hours spent fishing and that setlines allowed them to avoid having to stay up late fishing with a rod and reel. Most setliners that Dickinson interviewed identified their primary reasons were that they were interested in harvesting fish as opposed to fishing for sport, and that setlines were part of their independent lifestyle. Set lines are just more efficient at producing food. These sound like solid survival answers to me.

Set lines are designed to allow you to leave them unattended for hours; typically overnight. One caution is that the longer you leave your line unattended, the greater the chance your catch will turn into a meal for a larger fish or a snapping turtle and the more likely that any caught fish will expire on the line, making it unfit for eating.

For a fixed line, all that is required is something secure to anchor the shore end of your line, and a weight like a rock or piece of metal that you can throw to carry your line out to it's furthest extent. Two or three to as many as 5 baited lines come off the main line, and are spaced 5 – 10 feet apart. This will allow you to cover a lot of territory. You can quickly put 3, 4 or more of these lines into operation. Your success with unattended lines will not be as great as it would be if you were standing there, ready to set your hook at the right time. But 12 to 21 baited hooks will allow you to harvest a lot of fish, if there are any close to the shore line.

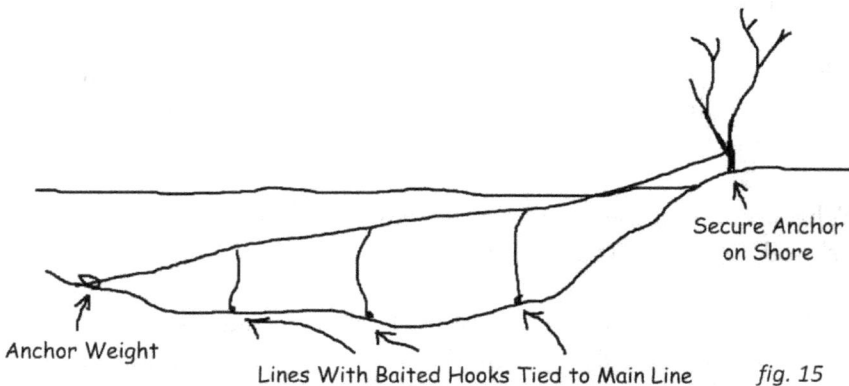

Secure Anchor on Shore

Anchor Weight

Lines With Baited Hooks Tied to Main Line   *fig. 15*

Once you get into open water, either a larger lake or even off shore, at the ocean side, you can use the same principal. You won't be able to use an onshore anchor, so you will need to make use of anchored floats to mark your line. Floats will make the line more visible. If you are concerned with visibility, you can get away with plastic bottles partially filled with water to allow them to sit lower in the water and not be so visible.

You need to ensure that you have a substantial weight securing your set line in place. A large body of water may mean you are not be as familiar with the correct or optimum spots for your set, so it makes sense to use a longer line and more baited hooks. Cut bait is the easiest way to go. The illustration below gives you a good idea of the kind of rig required. It is commonly used in commercial fishing.

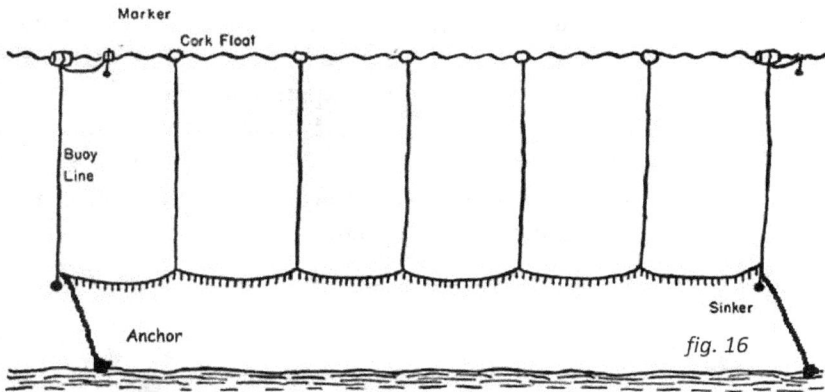

fig. 16

If you are in a completely unknown body of water, you will not know what depth is optimum. Your first set might want to look like the arrangement in figure 17.

This kind of a setup will maximize your exposure to fish, and your next set can focus on the depth that provided you with the greatest results.

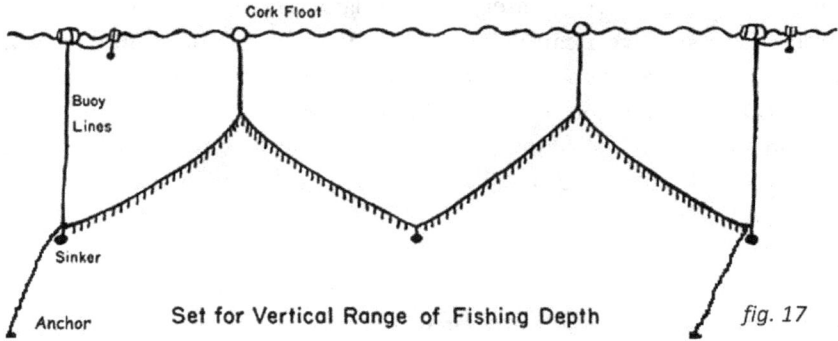

Set for Vertical Range of Fishing Depth   *fig. 17*

I will repeat that these illustrations are typical of commercial sets, so they show representations of hooks that are far more numerous than I suggest you run. These kinds of sets were typically put out in locations where the fishermen expected to encounter heavy schools of fish.

Trial and error is going to be necessary for you to find out your optimum set up. I don't know if you are fishing in Lake Erie, the Mississippi, or Otter Lake. But the principles I am describing have been successfully used for hundreds of years to take large numbers of fish. Ideally you want a set up that will allow you to reap a large harvest easily, quietly and such that your biggest concern is preserving your catch, not constantly going out to try again.

TROT LINES AND DROPLINES

Trotlines and droplines are heavy lines or cords with baited hooks attached at intervals by means of branch lines called snoods. A snood is a short length of line which is attached to the main line using a clip or swivel, (or a knot) with the hook at the other end. A trot line is typically fixed to shore at both ends. A trotline can be set so it covers the width of a channel, river, or stream with baited hooks and can be left unattended.

Whereas a trotline has a series of hooks suspended horizontally in the water, a dropline has a series of hooks suspended vertically in the water.

TROT LINES

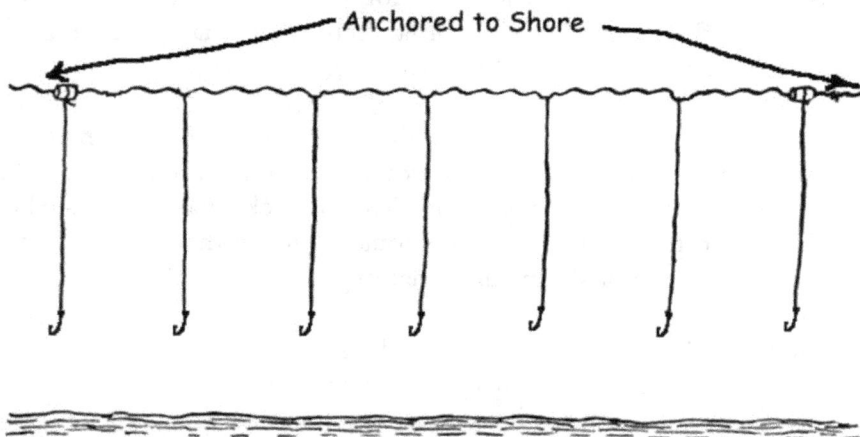

Anchored to Shore

fig 18

There are many ways to set a trotline, with most methods involving weights to hold the cord below the surface of the water. They are used for catching crabs or fish (particularly catfish). Trotlines are illegal in most jurisdictions unless you have a commercial license.

fig. 19

Constructing a trotline is quite simple. Basic supplies needed are fishing hooks, clamps (Figure19), swivels, fishing line, and a durable cord or lightweight rope used for the main line. Before constructing the trotline, it is a good idea to measure the span of the body of water being fished in order to give the main line an appropriate length.

Once this is done, branch lines are set along the main line by threading clamps on the line with swivels attached to the clamps. Fishing line is attached to the swivels and hooks are tied to the end of the fishing line.

It is important to make sure that the area where the line is to be set is free of swimmers, boaters, or other people on or near the water as it is difficult to detect where a trotline is while it is underwater. It is easy to get tangled in the line and for hooks to become embedded in a person's skin, making the need for proper marking of the line crucial. A float on each side of a section of channel is a good indication that a trotline has been set.

Setting the line consists of anchoring one end to one side of the channel, then leting the line out as you travel to the other side, baiting the hooks while this is being done. Trees or rocks make good anchor points for trotlines, but attention should be given that the line is not tied around rough or sharp edges that might cut through the line.

If the hook lines are left attached to the snood clamps, then it is very quick and easy to set up a trot line. Anchor your primary cord then (typically by boat) stretch it to your secondary anchor, attaching the baited lines with the clamps as you go. Attach the line to the final anchor and you are done. Check the line every couple of hours and replace bait or hooks and lines as required.

Once the line is set, the angler need only check periodically throughout the day to see if any fish have been caught. While checking the line, one can also replace bait, untangle as required, and retrieve any fish on the line.

Additionally, many localities that allow trotlines do not allow the use of live bait fish, particularly in areas with populations of largemouth bass or similar predator fish, as game fish caught on a trotline and left overnight can be severely injured or killed when attempting to escape.

TESTING

It is important to take note of what works and what doesn't as you go about refining your technique. An article that appeared in an issue of the *North American Journal of Fisheries Management* in 2002 reported on research that was done to determine the best methods of using trotlines for catfish sampling.

Extensive testing over two years revealed some important information. Authors John E. Arterburn and Charles R. Berry, Jr. stated:

> *"Channel catfish were 3.5 times more likely to be caught on hooks baited with cut common carp <u>Cyprinus carpio</u>, and flathead catfish were 28 times more likely to be caught on hooks baited with live black bullheads <u>Ameiurus melas</u>."*

It is worth noting that typical game fish, such as bass, walleye etc. will take live bait at a much higher rate than cut bait. In addition, gamefish catches will be much higher in spring and fall than in the summer. There is quite a difference in both cases.

The type of hook used was also important. As was location:

> *Seacircle hooks caught fewer catfish of either species than O'Shaughnessy or modified circle hooks. Channel type, water depth, and substrate type affected catches of flathead and channel catfish from the Big Sioux River, but did not influence catches of either species on the James River. The Big Sioux River had greater habitat variability, thereby increasing our chances of finding differences in trotline catches between habitat types.*

If you are counting on fishing for protein, you can see how critical it is to try different bait, hooks, locations and setups.

Overall the authors found that they harvested between 1 and 2 catfish for every 10 baited lines they put out, per night. The fish ranged in size from about 9" to almost 3 feet in length. Ten trotlines, with ten sets of baited hooks each could generate a lot of fish. If you maximized your sets as to bait and type of hook then fine-tuned depth and location, you could do even better.

DROP LINES

Drop lines have multiple hooks, in common with the other methods under discussion here, but they are vertical in their orientation (fig.20). Using a drop line you can fish at as many different depths as you have line to let out. This allows you to fish for different species as well as in different temperature zones.

Setting out half a dozen drop lines can fairly quickly give you a reasonable idea of where and at what depth you should be concentrating, based on what depths you get strikes..

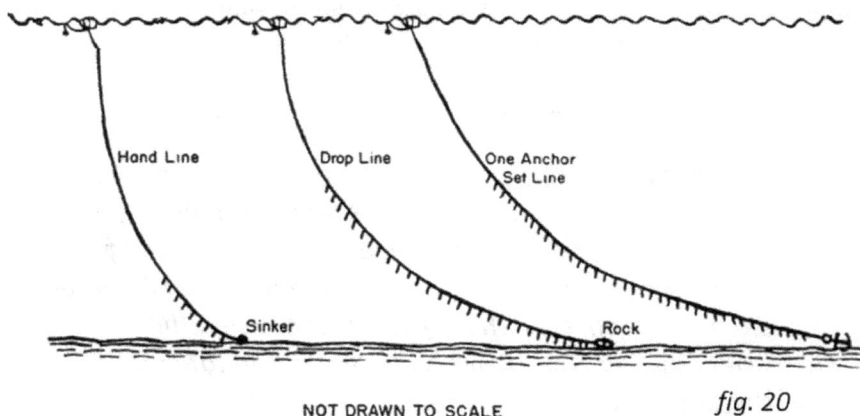

NOT DRAWN TO SCALE   fig. 20

Typically, drop lines are set so that the hook of one line cannot touch the hook of another line, to prevent the fish from getting tangled up in multiple lines or getting tangled in lines with other fish already on the line. This might mean, for example, using lines just over 3 feet long and having the lines spaced at 6 foot intervals. It is also best to avoid setting lines directly over stumps, branches or other obstacles that might cause the fish to get tangled.

Figure 20 shows lines typical of offshore rigs used in coastal waters, but the principle works for inland lakes. It is a simple way of checking out prime depth for your set.

If you are putting a drop line into a lake or river channel, you would have fewer hooks than shown unless you were dealing with a very deep lake.

Weighting the line is a matter of personal preference. In areas along rivers and channels with strong currents, large weights may be added to keep the line from being pulled close to the surface as the water flows past the line. The speed and force of the current will dictate exactly what sized weight to use.

I will repeat that I am talking about the use of trot lines, setlines and drop lines in a survival or post-SHTF situation with all of these methods. Although many of these methods are legal in some locations, for some species of fish (notably commercial fishing and/or when used for catfish), they are illegal in many others. When used legally, typically you are required to use marker buoys and/or warning flags at either end of your set.

LIMB LINES

Limb lines are used for catfish throughout the southern US but the concept is a good one and can easily be used for other species. Ideally you have access to a boat. Look for a bush or tree growing on the bank of a river or small lake with a branch that extends out over the water. Check out the illustration below.

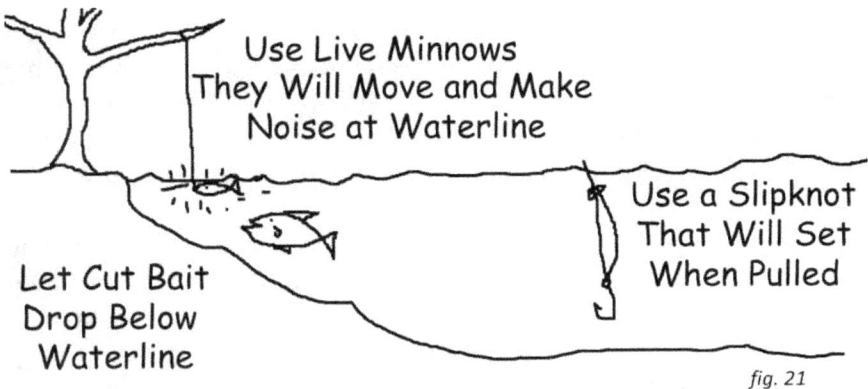

Use Live Minnows
They Will Move and Make
Noise at Waterline

Use a Slipknot
That Will Set
When Pulled

Let Cut Bait
Drop Below
Waterline

fig. 21

Look for slow moving water in a section of the river or a small lake where the bottom drops off relatively quickly. Find a nice supple green tree or shrub branch that extends out over the water. A water logged section of tree with a limb that extends out of the water also works well.

Your fishing line should just reach below the water surface for live bait. Keeping them on or near the surface will allow their movement to attract attention from below and the result will be larger fish being caught. Your line should drop a little below the water's surface for cut bait.

Check your placement and line length to ensure that any fish that gets hooked will not be able to get the line entangled in other limbs or obstructions. This is one of the advantages of a limb line over a set line attached to a shoreline anchor and a weight thrown out to extend you line. With a limb line the movement is vertical. You are far less likely to get hooked on underwater structure or vegetation because you are not hauling your line in with a horizontal motion.

The best way to make maximum use of the supple and flexible limb you have tied off to will be to use a slip knot, tied about 8" – 12" above the hook. This will allow the target fish to take the bait and move away, feeling some slight resistance. This will encourage it to lunge away from the resistance, setting the hook.

With a boat, in the right kind of environment, you can set half a dozen of these in very little time. I don't know your conditions or region or what time of year you are doing this, so you will have to do some trial and error. Put them out early in the morning then come back and check them later a couple of hours later. Put them out last thing in the evening, and then check them first thing in the morning. It won't take you long before you find out what works in your area.

If each line has a dowel at the end, it can be attached by simply taking several wraps around a branch, a wrap around the line itself and then reversing direction for a couple of more wraps around the branch, leaving the dowel hanging and secured. When you pack up, just wrap your line and hook around the dowels, set the hook tip in the end of the dowel, and you are set and ready for next time.

JUG LINES

A jug line is a length of line with a baited hook that is weighted and suspended from a float or "jug." Think two litre plastic bottle and you've got a good idea what the set up would look like. Jug lines are frequently set out twenty at a time. They are typically set out in the evening and then checked in the morning. The weights need to be heavy enough to keep them in place.

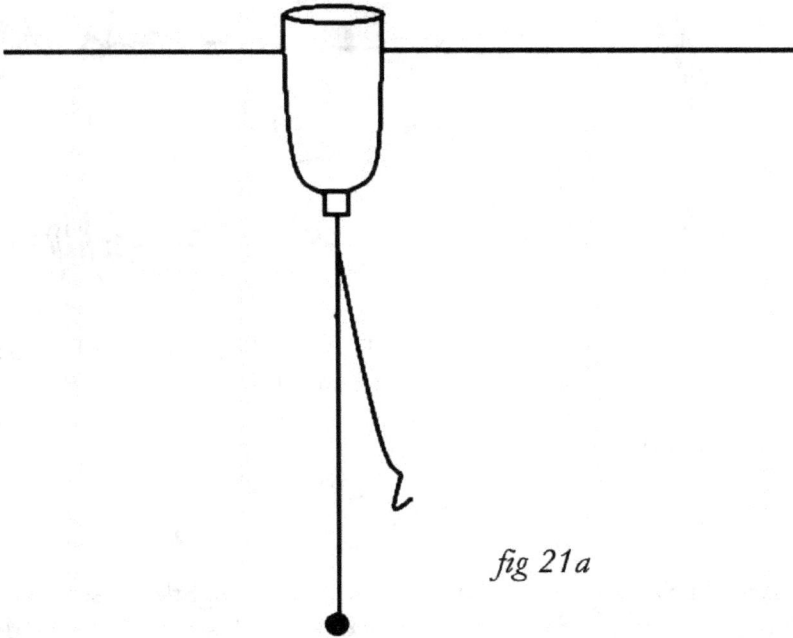

fig 21a

STAKEOUT LINE

A stakeout is a specialized type of trotline. It is designed to be invisible from shore. It is recommended in military survival manuals because of its unobtrusive nature. While you may not be a downed pilot behind enemy lines trying to avoid capture, you may be in a situation in which you don't wish your fishing efforts to be noticed.

To construct a stakeout line drive two supple saplings into the bottom of the lake, pond, or stream with their tops just below the water surface; if you can find some underwater growth, or a submerged log or stump, so much the better. Tie a cord between

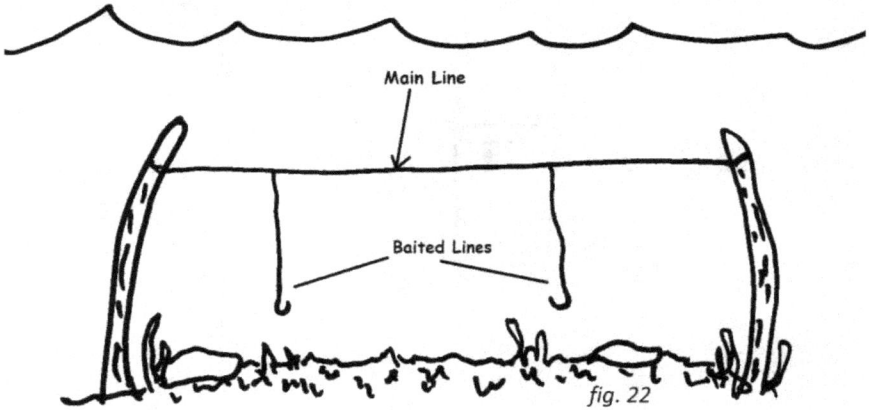

fig. 22

them and slightly below the surface. Tie short lines with hooks to this cord, ensuring that they cannot wrap around the poles or each other. They should also not slip along the long cord. Bait the hooks And check frequently.

MONTAGNAIS NIGHTLINE

Similar to a Stakeout or Jug line was a type of nightline used by the Montagnais people of the St. Lawrence River. A simple construction generally used with a single hook and left out overnight, this set up had a low visibility and depended on the user knowing where it had been set so that it could be checked easily. If you could not see the stick poking up above the water, you knew you had caught something.

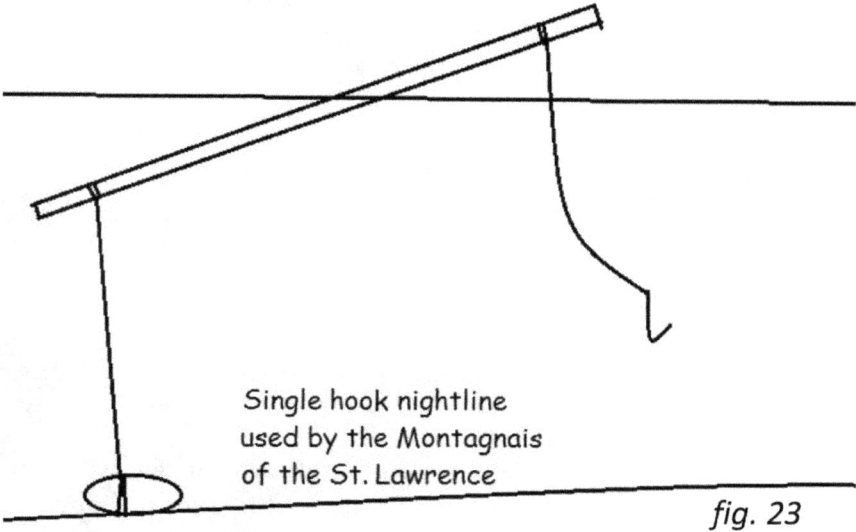

Single hook nightline
used by the Montagnais
of the St. Lawrence

fig. 23

The limb line, jug line, stakeout and Montagnais nightline are all examples of individual sets that can be easily multiplied to improve your chances of catching fish. You can profitably spend a chunk of time assembling and constructing multiple sets at once, before going out to put them in place. While you are waiting for them to work, you can get busy with whatever else needs doing to improve your chances of survival. Collecting material and constructing equipment to help preserve your catch is discussed in the final section of this book.

5 NETS

GILL NETS

In a survival situation, if a gill net is not available, you can make one using paracord or similar material. Remove the sheath from the paracord and tie it between two trees. You can use your paracord to frame the whole net when you are done. Attach several of the inner

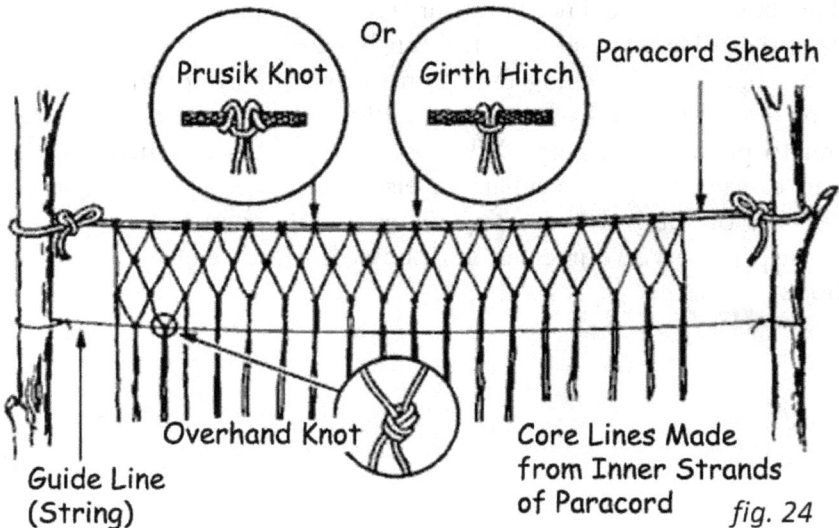

Prusik Knot

Or

Girth Hitch

Paracord Sheath

Guide Line
(String)

Overhand Knot

Core Lines Made
from Inner Strands
of Paracord

fig. 24

strands to the main sheath line by doubling them over and tying them with prusik knots or girth hitches, forming your core lines. The length of the desired net and the size of the mesh determine the number of core lines used and the space between them.

Starting at one end of the sheath, tie the second and the third core lines together using an overhand knot. Then tie the fourth and fifth, sixth and seventh, and so on, until you reach the last core line. You should now have all core lines tied in pairs with a single core line hanging at each end. Start the second row with the first core line, tie it to the second, the third to the fourth, and so on.

To keep the rows even and to regulate the size of the mesh, tie a guideline to the trees. Position the guideline on the opposite side of the net you are working on. Move the guideline down after completing each row. The lines will always hang in pairs and you always tie a cord from one pair to a cord from an adjoining pair. Continue tying rows until the net is the desired width. Thread a paracord sheath along the bottom of the net to strengthen it.

The size of the opening in your net determines the size of the fish you catch. If your mesh size is too small, you will capture larger quantities of small fish. This may not be a bad thing in a survival situation. For ongoing harvest, a mesh size of 4 cm (1 ½") is about right. Almost all of the fish caught within the net will make a decent meal in themselves.

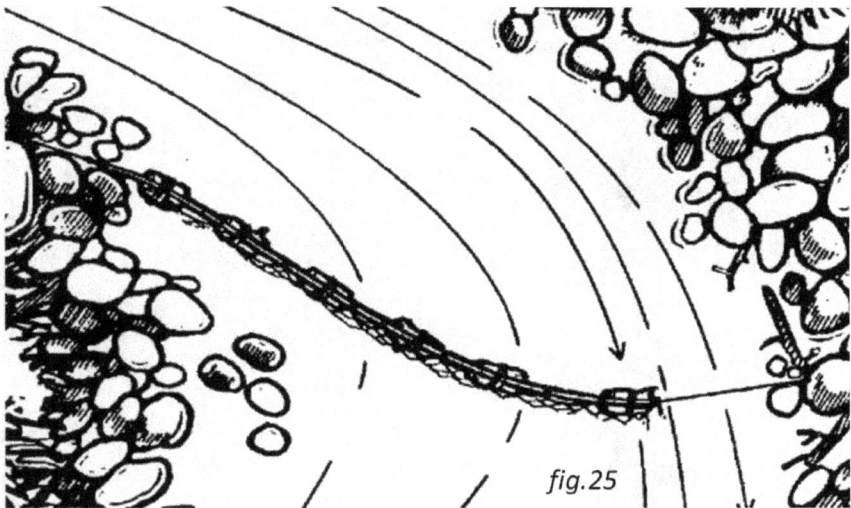

fig.25

You should check the net a couple of times a day. You need to not only collect any fish that are caught, but also remove debris that gets tangled in the net due to the flow of water through it.

Testing by the State of Louisiana in 1981 indicated that monofilament line gill nets had a larger harvest in fish numbers and pounds than gill nets made from nylon. I couldn't find reports of any other tests, so you can go ahead and make your choice. I think I would use monofilament.

SEINE NETS

A seine net is similar to a gill net except that is moved through the water. The illustrations below (Figures 26, 27) show a seine net being operated by three individuals. In this application fish are corralled by the seine net, and harvested with a dip net.

fig. 26

Above, working a stream, and on the next page you can see the same type of net being used on a pond.

As you can see, seine nets typically have a series of floats on the top edge and weights on the bottom edge.

fig. 27

DIP NETS

fig. 28

I don't think I have to say a lot about dip nets. Aside from helping land your catch if using a rod and line, they can be used for catching fish from weirs, from stream bed rock traps, while wading in shallow water, during annual runs up creeks and rivers, on the sea or lake side or, as discussed on the previous page, with a seine net.

There are dip nets made specifically for smelt runs, with telescoping handles as well.

fig. 29

THROW NETS

Do a search online for "bait cast net" to see some options for throw nets. Typically used along a shallow shoreline or sandy bottom, cast nets have been the ready standby of Pacific fishermen for centuries but have also been used on inland waterways and rivers. Check below for a couple of examples.

fig 30

It is not hard to use these nets but it does require practice. It is a little complicated to explain. And it would be a waste of time unless you have one to practice with. I suggest you go to YouTube and search for "How to Throw a Cast Net." There are numerous examples.

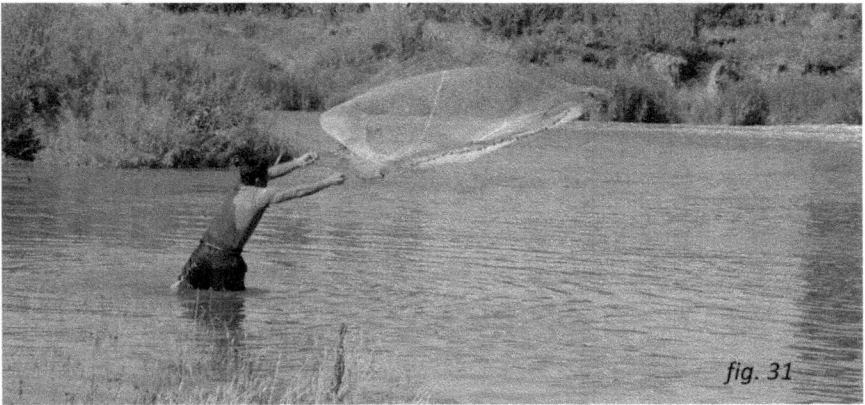

fig. 31

Check out the "Resources" page at the back of the book for some links to examples, and some specific search phrases to use. Make sure to check out "Top 10 Cast Net and Bait Catching Videos." You will see some amazing hauls. If you decide you want to use live bait on your trotline, a cast net is a quick way to collect some, if you have a nice smooth sandy or mud bottom

LIFT NETS

I can remember my brother and I going lift netting along with my Dad and his brothers to the side of the Welland Canal during the smelt run in the 1950's. Their nets had strong supports with long poles attached and my Dad and my uncles would lower large nets into the water, and then crank them up with a windlass. The nets would be full of smelt. Somewhat similar to the rig below, except we were on the edge of the canal, not in a boat.

fig 32

I've gone out myself, from a beach on the shore of Lake Huron, in hip waders with a hand dip net, with smelt sized mesh, and gathered my own fair share of freshwater goodness. It is not difficult to attach a net to a long pole to extend your reach for fish harvest. Putting together a lift net is slightly more complicated, but if you are in a location where it would be useful, particularly during a run, there is nothing quite like it.

Here a couple of different iterations from developing nations that are both quite doable. The first is quite simple. Ideally you have a prefabricated net. All that is required is two poles, lengths of conduit or even two by fours. Sink one of them in the ground. Put a hinge mechanism in place. It could be some lashing, a bolt through both pieces and held on with a nut, or something more elaborate. It is a simple matter to lower the net. Wait, or cast some bait on the surface, and then lift.

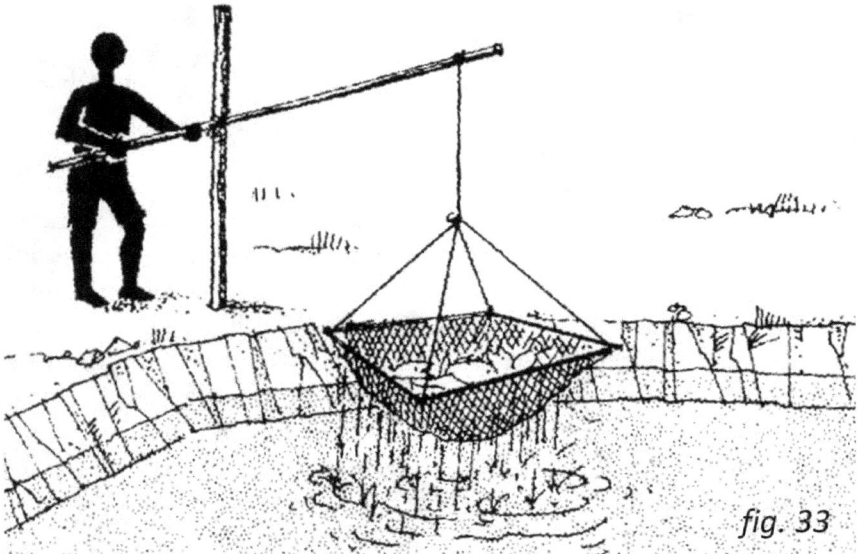

fig. 33

An alternative requiring only one pole and a bit of care is on the next page (Figure 34). The hinge is attached to a pole or post at water level and from your higher vantage point you simply haul in on a rope.

The net swings over dry land or the side of a dock or wharf and you can gather the fish. This arrangement allows you to reach a little further out into the body of water you are harvesting from. A set up like this and a several day regimen of chumming could turn into a nice haul of fish. During the annual run, when fish are travelling up stream, you could quickly pull in hundreds of pounds of fish for drying and salting.

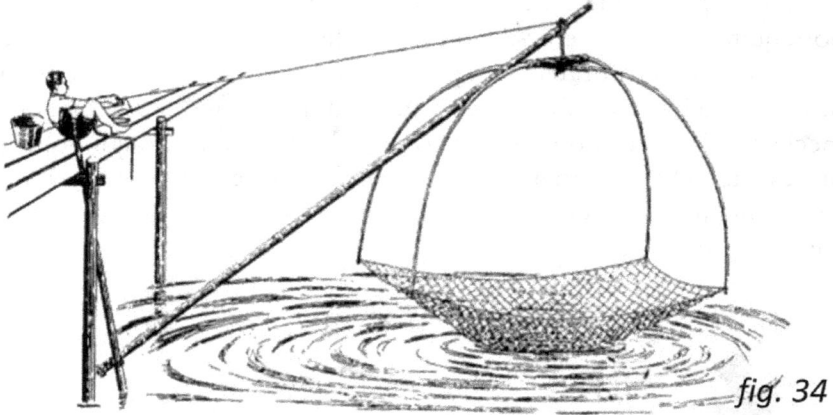

fig. 34

EXPEDIENT NETS

There are lots of options when it comes to expedient nets. Some of the many ideas that come to mind are hammocks, mosquito netting from your bed, mosquito hats, shirts etc., mesh shirts, campers dining tents, the mosquito netting on most family tent doors and windows, badminton or volleyball nets, large chunks of window screen or rolls of window screening material, screen covers for garden ponds, mesh to protect fruit trees or berry patches and probably more I haven't thought of. Any of these can be fashioned into, at the very least, dip nets for catching minnows, which can then be used as bait or cooked and eaten as they are.

There are all kinds of nets, and various ways to use them. And I could outline here exactly how to construct them. The method shown for the gill net can be used for many of the others. You can also use expedient materials as suggested above.

The truth is, given the costs involved, and the superiority of virtually any net you can buy, if you are concerned about prepping for complete disaster, go ahead and just buy some, and pack them away for a SHTF day.

Go online and put "fishing net," or "gill net," or "smelt net" or "bait cast net" into the search field. Considering the cost, size and weight of any of these, why wouldn't you grab a couple of different types?

Just make sure you don't put "fish net" into the search function by mistake. You get a whole different kind of result.

How much have you invested in your food preps? Just a fraction invested in commercially available nets or trotlines could have a far bigger impact in your survival than a months' worth of stored food.

6 FISH TRAPS

NET TRAP

You may trap fish in multiple ways. The method of using a net is illustrated below. It doesn't need much explanation.

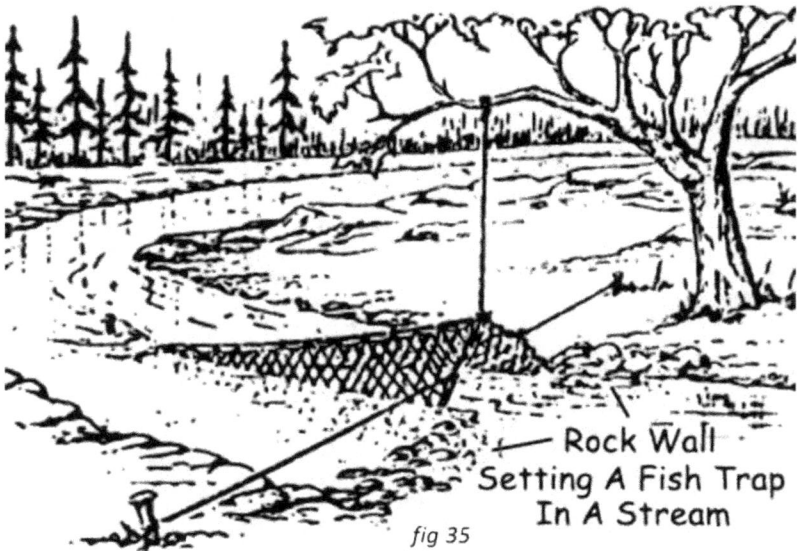

Rock Wall
Setting A Fish Trap
In A Stream

fig 35

BASKET TRAP

Fish baskets are another method. You construct them by lashing several sticks together with cord or wire into a funnel shape. You close the top, and leave a hole in your funnel large enough for the fish to swim through. You can construct this kind of trap easily with Wire mesh. See Figure 38.

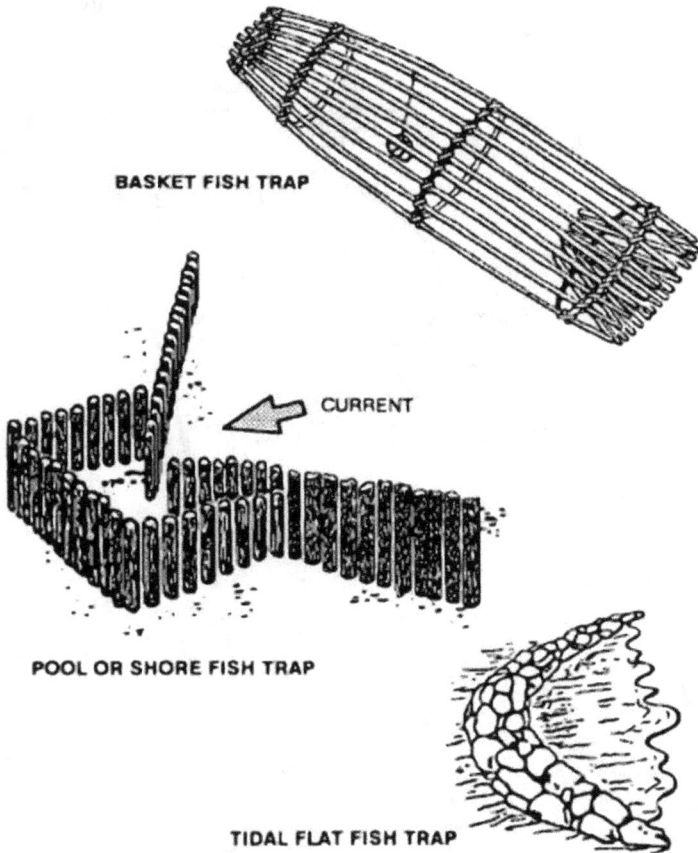

BASKET FISH TRAP

CURRENT

POOL OR SHORE FISH TRAP

TIDAL FLAT FISH TRAP

fig. 36

You can also use traps to catch saltwater fish, as schools regularly approach the shore with the incoming tide and often move parallel to the shore. Pick a location at high tide and build the trap at low tide. On rocky shores, use natural rock pools. On coral islands, use natural pools on the surface of reefs by blocking the openings as the tide recedes. On sandy shores, use sandbars and the ditches they enclose. Build the trap as a low stone wall extending outward into the water and forming an angle with the shore.

WEIR TRAPS

Weirs are arrangements of stones or vertically set posts that funnel fish into a pen where they can be collected more easily, either with spears, nets or baskets.

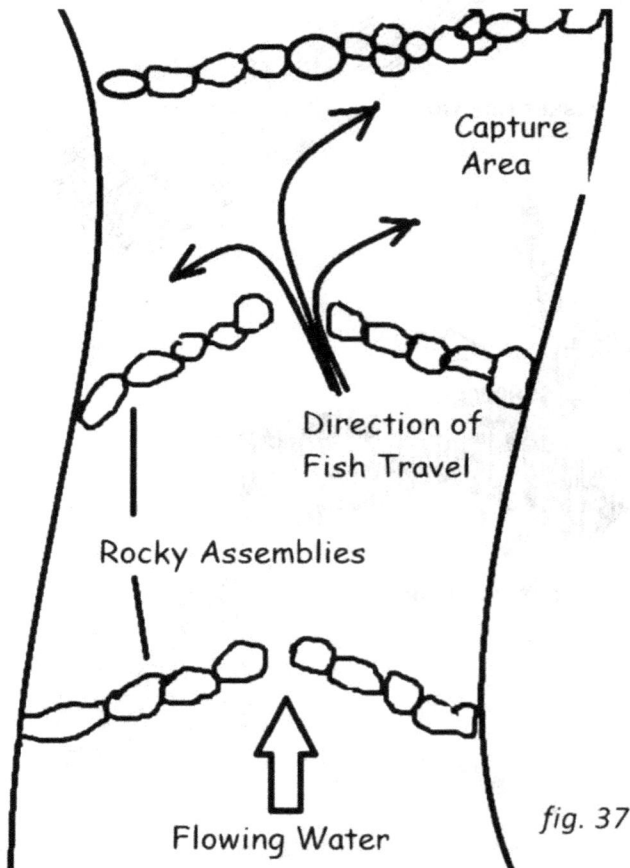

Capture Area

Direction of Fish Travel

Rocky Assemblies

Flowing Water

fig. 37

Weirs can be set in tidal areas or across rivers. An example below is pictured in Figure 37.

WIRE MESH TRAP

It is ridiculously easy to fabricate a wire mesh trap. Use the basket fish trap in figure 36 as your guide. All you need is some wire mesh; chicken wire or a smaller mesh would work. Look for anything that is 1" x 1" or maybe 1" x ½". If you go much smaller, you will be able to harvest smaller fish, but the weight of the trap becomes greater. There is a trade-off. Go with the lightest gauge wire you can find. However light it is, your trapped fish will not be able to break out.

There is no point in making a small trap. Make it 3' to 4' long. If you can find a cylindrical tomato cage, you have got a perfectly good frame.

Fabricating an easily opened hatch on one end, and a funnel entrance on the other is not difficult. Throw some bait inside and check periodically. Because you are not leaving your catch impaled on a hook, die off rates will be low. See the image below for the general shape to shoot for. Check the following pages for several different ideas including fish traps made from 2 litre soda bottles.

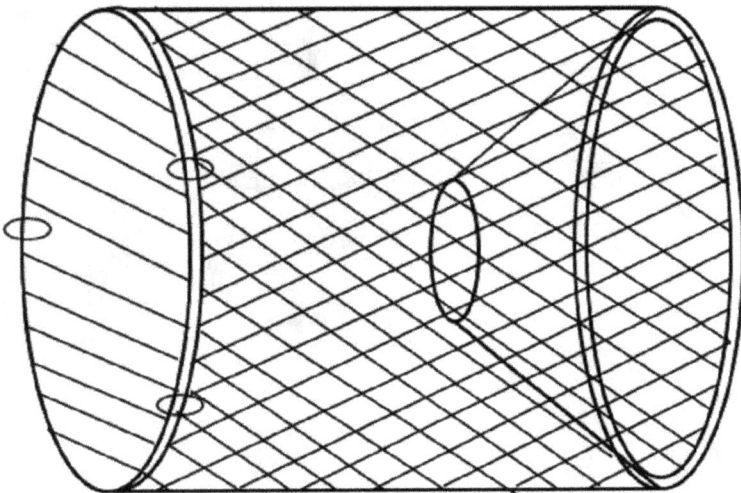

fig. 38

fig 39

Tidal Mesh Funnel Trap   fig. 40

SODA BOTTLE TRAP

In Haikou, China, local people make bottle traps with small, glass jars. Local craftspeople produce a variant made from a two-litre soda bottle. This type has an inverted funnel made by cutting off the top of the bottle a few centimeters down the neck, and making vertical cuts downward. This produces tabs which are then be pushed inward, producing the inverted funnel shape. A stone is attached to the side of the bottle, and several meters of line are provided. Numerous holes are drilled through the bottle to allow water to enter and escape.

Fig 41

8 PROJECTILE/STRIKE

A different category of fishing involves forcing a projectile into the flesh of the fish or striking the fish as a means of harvest. All of these methods involve proactive action on the part of the person doing the catching, as opposed to letting the fish take a bait or wander into a trap or net based on their own movements or inclination. I will admit it is a loose category, but it allows me to group a diverse set of methods under a specific heading.

SPEARFISHING

If you are near shallow water waist deep or less, where the fish are large and plentiful, you can spear them. To make a spear, cut a long, straight sapling. Sharpen the end to a point or attach a knife, jagged piece of bone, or sharpened metal for your point.

You can also make a spear by splitting the shaft a few inches down from the end and inserting a piece of wood to act as a spreader.

You then sharpen the two separated halves to points. To spear fish, find an area where fish either gather, where there is a fish run or set up a fish trap that directs them to the killing ground. Place the spear point into the water and slowly move it toward the fish. Then, with a sudden push, impale the fish on the stream bottom. Do not try to lift the fish with the spear, as it with probably slip off and you will lose it; hold the spear with one hand and grab and hold the fish with the other.

An alternative method is to arrange your spear so that it acts to grab the fish while impaling it, as in Figure 41a.

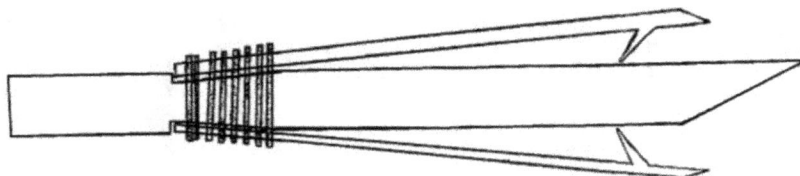

fig. 41a

Do not throw the spear, especially if the point is a knife. You cannot afford to lose a knife in a survival situation.

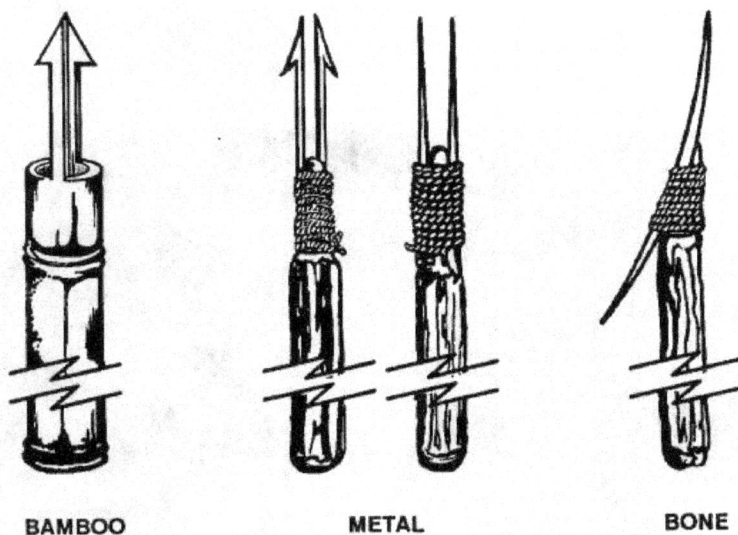

BAMBOO   METAL   BONE

fig. 42

Something you need to be aware of when spearfishing, bow fishing or any other activity that requires you to physically contact a fish from some distance away is refraction. When light passes from one medium to another (from water to air) the path of the light bends. The actual location of the fish will vary as the angle changes. The smaller the angle between the visual path and the surface of the water, the further away the fish will appear to be.

Your best bet is to be spearing (or shooting your arrow) almost straight down. When light passes from one medium to another at an angle of 90 degrees, there is no bending.

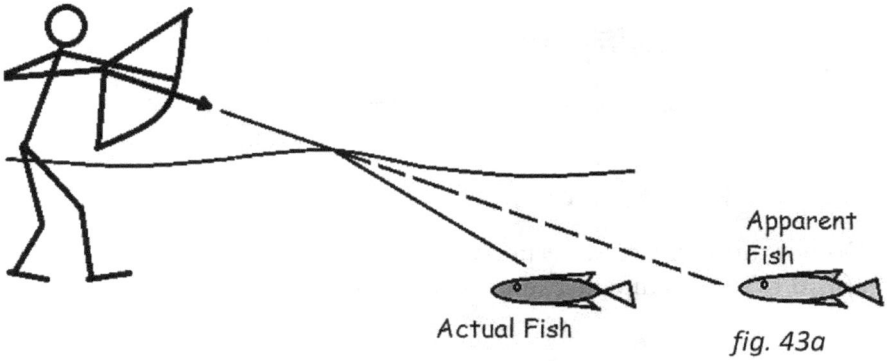

Apparent Fish

Actual Fish

fig. 43a

fig. 44

Spearfishing with a light at night is effective with virtually all fish in virtually all places. Fish are blinded by the light and don't see the approaching spear hunter. You need to move slowly with as little splashing or disturbance as possible. This technique is best used by working upstream in a river or stream, or from a boat in the shallows of a larger body of water.

fig. 45

Below is an example of Inuit using spears in a stone weir trap.(Figure 45a)

fig. 45a

Gig fishing in Florida from a boat. (Figure 45b) This allows the spear fisherman to get closer to a straight downward thrust, eliminating refraction as an issue.

45b

BOWFISHING

When I was a young teenager, my brother and I would go out bow fishing for suckers and carp with homemade rigs. We had cheap fibre glass bows, but the arrows, harpoon heads, and line reels were all contraptions that we made up ourselves. And during the spring run, we had no trouble catching all the fish we wanted.

fig. 46

There's not a lot has to be said about this method other than you need to be able to see the fish, and as in Figure 46 above, you need to learn where to aim. If you are already into archery, you might want to consider purchasing the appropriate attachments for your bow. Alternatively, buy a cheap, second hand recurve bow and fabricate some homemade gear. I recommend going to Google or YouTube and searching for "DIY Bowfishing."

CHOP FISHING

At night, you can use a light to attract fish. Then, armed with a machete or any long, narrow object with some weight, you can gather fish using the blunt side of the blade to strike them. Do not use the

fig. 47

sharp side as you will cut them in two pieces and end up losing some of the fish.

This is a process that works well with more than one person. You need to hold the light and attack the fish while the other person picks the fish up with a net and transports them to a container on shore.

SNAGGING

Snagging a fish is the process of setting a hook into its body in any method other than by generating a strike on the bait or lure. Typically poachers who practice snagging use long leaders and heavier braided line. Snagging works best when there are a number of fish in a specific location. A fish that has been hooked in the mouth will follow a set pattern of moves, involving trying to run away. Putting pressure on your line will turn its head and cause it to run in a different direction than it wants to. A fish that is hooked in the body will be able to pull directly away from you, exerting a lot more pressure on your line. That's why a long leader and heavier line is required.

It is possible to use multiple hooks on a single line. In his book "Survival Poaching" Ragnar Benson advises tying the hooks to the line about 3" apart. He suggests securing a piece of rubber tubing to the end of the hook line with a heavy enough piece of lead wire attached to it so that you can cast the line out. Then start working the river or stream. Cast out, wait for half a minute or so, then jerk the line sharply enough to snag any fish in contact with it. Keep reeling it in until you have covered the area, then cast it out again, or move on. He doesn't offer detailed explanations or a diagram of the line set up, but I'm guessing the rubber tubing and lead wire would help eliminate getting caught on rocks etc. and help prevent snapping the line. Treble hooks, by their nature, would be more effective at snagging a fish than regular hooks and should be used with this method.

GAFF FISHING

Gaff fishing is essentially snagging, with a large hooked tool, instead of a fishing line and hook. It can be particularly effective in locations where fish gather or during a fish run. The gaff must be on a long pole so that you can maneuver it below the fish or on the far side of the fish from your position. The point must be very sharp so that it penetrates the skin. Gaffing from above is easier because the less protected, softer tissue on the fish's belly is exposed to the point of the hook.

fig. 48

Once the fish is out of the water, its own weight will tend to keep it secure on the gaff. This method is limited by the reach of your gaff pole and the visibility in the water. Nonetheless, given the correct conditions, a gaff and a long pole has the ability to pull in some big fish, without a high degree of skill.

9 SNARING

SNARING FISH

It is quite possible to snare fish with a length of wire attached to a pole. It requires practice, like anything else. I have come across one report of a first timer carefully slipping the snare over a big sucker and then giving a mighty jerk to flip it on the bank of the stream.

> *"I was thunder-struck when I discovered that the fine wire of the snare had cut the fish completely in halves, and as the muddy water, stirred up by the commotion beneath, rolled away downstream, I beheld one-half of the 'mud sucker' with the puckering mouth still moving, and the other half with its tail flapping in the water beneath."*

Your snare wire needs to be a little lighter than rabbit snare wire. In Ontario, where I live the regulations call for rabbit snare wire to be 22 gauge and copper, so something a little lighter than that.

Ease the loop of your snare around the fish by moving it slowly through the water from the upstream side until you have slipped it over the head and past the gills. Then quickly lift the end of your pole, tightening the snare around the fish's body. Hopefully you don't cut the fish in two.

This obviously requires you to be able to see the fish so you can position the wire around it. Polarized sunglasses would be an asset when using this method or many of the other fish harvesting methods discussed in this book.

SNARING CRABS OR CRAYFISH

This is a pretty simple method of collecting some fresh crustacean protein. It is nothing more than a wire cage that you fill with bait (cut fish) and it has multiple snares attached to the outside, generally about six of them. Crabs or crayfish are attracted to the bait and one or more of their legs get caught.

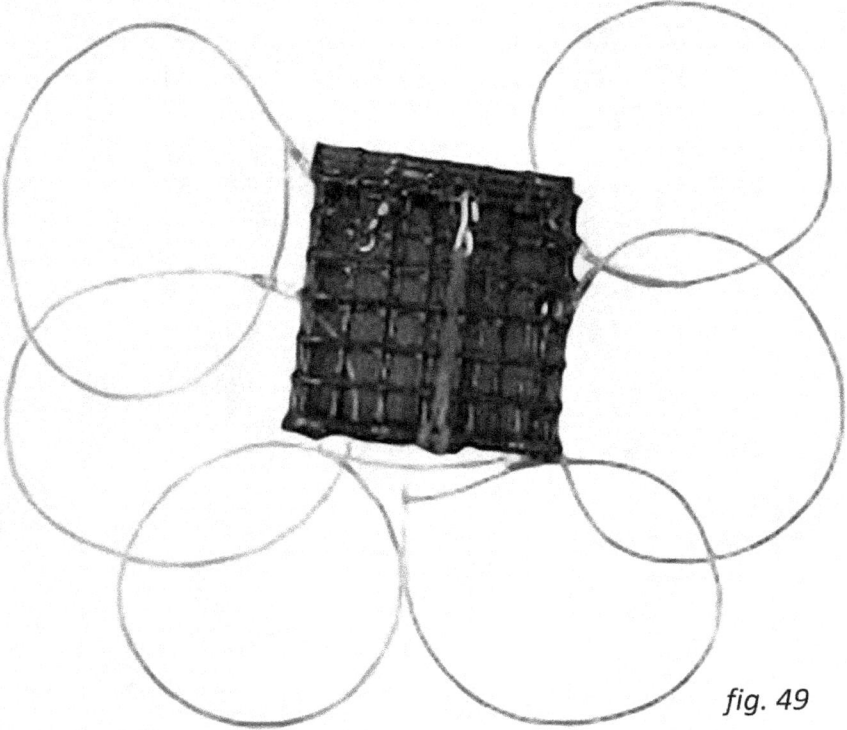

fig. 49

These are typically meant to be cast out from the seashore with a rod. You wait until you feel movement, and then haul them in. Do a Google Image search for "Crab Snare" and you will come up with several variations.

I have had a few shore lunches of fresh crayfish, caught the old fashioned way with fingers and a bucket. Snaring is definitely an easier way to go. A crab trap, built on a smaller scale might work very well. Actually commercial crayfish traps can be bought that look very much like the chicken wire fish trap illustration a few pages back. This is something that you could also fabricate yourself.

My personal experience with catching crayfish was that about 30 minutes work along a shallow, 15 cm – 30 cm (6" -12") deep gravel bottom stream with a pail and a quick hand was enough to provide a decent lunch for two.

If you have ever fed wild birds over the winter, then you have probably seen the wire suet containers that are hung out in winter to provide a snack for hungry chirpers. If you have one around the house, you already have a bait holder for a crab or crayfish snare. It doesn't take much effort to attach half a dozen snare loops to the suet holder; then you are in business. You can also easily fabricate a trap from simple wire mesh. Check out the resource page at the end of this book for links to several YouTube videos demonstrating fabrication.

10 STUNNING

There are several different methods used around the world to cause fish to become stunned or to otherwise lose their ability to flee. This is a loose grouping that work by many different mechanisms, from the simple to the technologically advanced, but all have the commonality of allowing people to collect fish simply by hand picking or netting after they come to the surface of the water.

FISH POISON

Catching fish by using poison is relatively common around the world and has been practiced by indigenous groups for thousands of years. Most poisons work quickly. It enables you to catch several fish at one time, multiplying your effectiveness. Some plants that grow in warm regions of the world contain rotenone, a substance that stuns or kills cold-blooded animals but does not harm persons who eat the animals. The best place to use rotenone, or rotenone-producing plants, is in ponds or the headwaters of small streams containing fish.

Rotenone works quickly on fish in water 21 degrees C (70 degrees F) or above. The fish rise helplessly to the surface. It works slowly in water 10 to 21 degrees C (50 to 70 degrees F) and is ineffective in water below 10 degrees C (50 degrees F). The following plants, used as indicated, will stun or kill fish:

Anamirta cocculus (Figure 50). This woody vine grows in southern Asia and on islands of the South Pacific. Crush the bean-shaped seeds and throw them in the water.

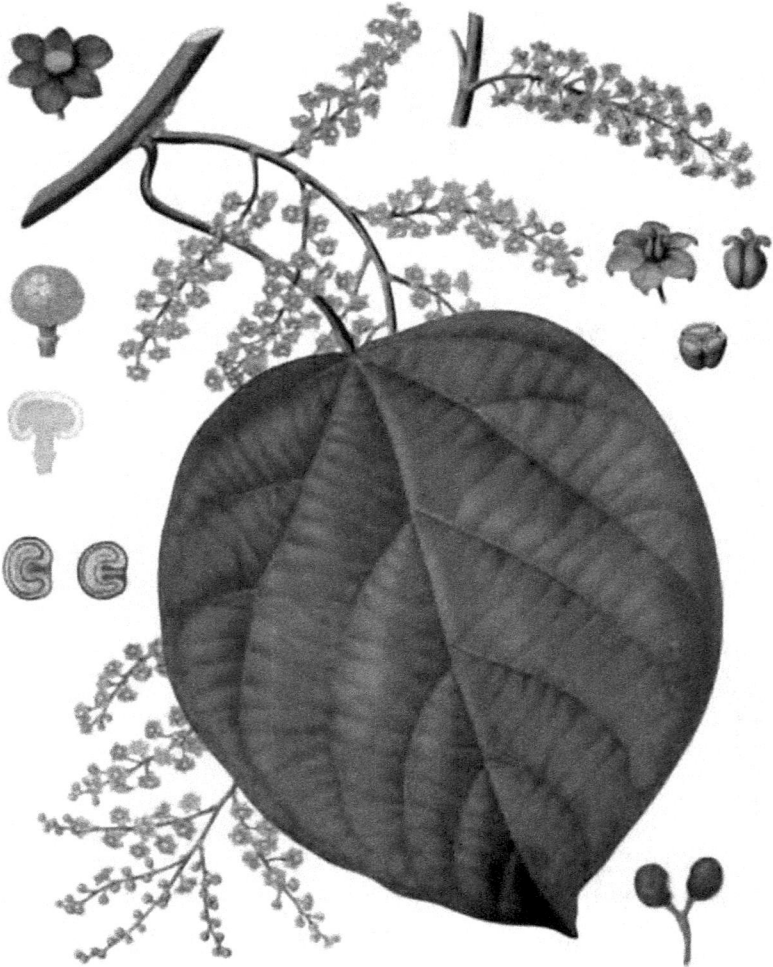

fig. 50

Barringtonia(Figure 51). These large trees grow near the sea in Malaya and parts of Polynesia. They bear a fleshy one-seeded fruit. Crush the seeds and bark and throw into the water.

By Tau'olunga - Own work, CC BY-SA 2.5, https://commons.wikimedia.org/w/index.php?curid=1951944   fig. 51

Black Walnut *uglans nigra* (Figure 52)

Black walnut is found throughout the eastern United States and into Southern Ontario. Placing the husks of the nut in a bag, then beating them and throwing the bag into a body of slow moving water will release an agent which stuns fish and will bring them to the surface.

fig. 52

Butternut *Juglans cinerea* (Figure 53)

The distribution range of the butternut extends east to New Brunswick, and from southern Quebec west to Minnesota, south to northern Alabama and southwest to northern Arkansas.

fig. 53

It is absent from most of the Southern United States. The species also proliferates at middle elevations (about 2,000 ft or 610 m above sea level) in the Columbia River basin, Pacific Northwest; as an off-site species.

Croton tiglium (Figure 54). This shrub or small tree grows in waste areas on islands of the South Pacific. It bears seeds in three angled capsules. Crush the seeds and throw them into the water.

fig. 54

Derris eliptica(Figure 55). This large genus of tropical shrubs and woody vines is the main source of commercially produced rotenone. Grind the roots into a powder and mix with water. Throw a large quantity of the mixture into the water.

fig. 55

By Forest & Kim Starr, CC BY 3.0, https://commons.wikimedia.org/w/index.php?curid=6108603

fig. 56

Duboisia (Figure 56). This shrub grows in Australia and bears white clusters of flowers and berrylike fruit. Crush the plants and throw them into the water.

Tephrosia (Figure 57/58). This species of small shrubs, which bears beanlike pods, grows throughout the tropics. Crush or bruise bundles of leaves and stems and throw them into the water.

By James Steakley - Own work, CC BY-SA 3.0, https://commons.wikimedia.org/w/index.php?curid

fig. 57

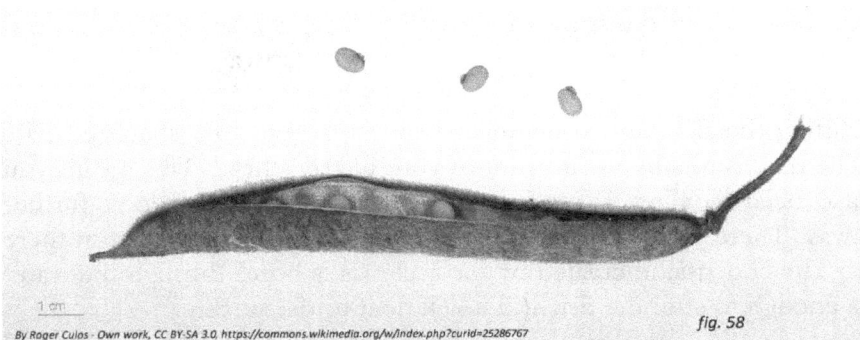

By Roger Culos - Own work, CC BY-SA 3.0, https://commons.wikimedia.org/w/index.php?curid=25286767

fig. 58

Lime. Not the plant, but the commercial powder. You can get lime from commercial sources and in agricultural areas that use large quantities of it. You may produce your own by burning coral or seashells. Throw the lime into the water.

MUD STIRRING

A method used in different places around the world is effective in small ponds or quiet waters in a stream where there is a muddy bottom. It works well if there is a slow current. The harvester takes a position up stream of the fish and starts stirring the water. Once the density of mud reaches a certain level the gills of the fish will not be able to extract sufficient oxygen from the water and they will begin to suffocate. This will cause them to rise to the surface where they can be gathered by means of a dip net or picked up by hand.

CONCUSSION TECHNIQUE

Most people have heard of using dynamite or hand grenades to go fishing. I am not going to go into any of the details of this method, since there are much safer ways to harvest. One that was completely unfamiliar to me until I started this book is bullet fishing.

In fish shooting you take your side arm of choice, find a nice stable location that can give you a reasonable view of your prey (a perch in a tree located on the bank of a river or lake, a boat or even a "fish blind") and wait for a likely target to swim your way.

Hitting the fish with your bullet is likely to lead to a shattered fish. The trick is to aim just in front of your quarry's head. This means you also need to allow for refraction, which makes a fish look further away. There more directly overhead you are, the less refraction there is. The concussion created by the bullet as is bores through the water is enough to stun the fish and it will float to the surface.

Ice hammering is a technique that is reported from northern Europe as early as the 1700's. Fish that gathered under ice in relatively shallow water were stunned when the ice above them was struck with large wooden mallets. The ice was subsequently opened up and the stunned fish were collected by hand. There are numerous variations on this technique but they are all based on the same principle as any of these concussion methods; shock waves propagating through water.

In one method of using the concussion technique, large stones that are lying in the water, but protruding from it, are stuck as strongly as possible with a sledge hammer. The hammer strike sends a shock wave through the water temporarily stunning nearby fish which are then collected by hand or with nets.

ELECTRO-FISHING

Electro-fishing is the practice of harvesting fish through the mechanism of passing an electric current through the water to stun the fish. Generally, affected fish float to the surface, then it is a simple process to collect them with a dip net.

fig. 59

The setup requires an anode, a cathode and a source of electricity. Electrofishing setups can be found that are suitable for use on a boat or that are small enough to be available in a backpack mode (Figure 59). In the boat system, the hull of the boat acts as a cathode, and the anode is dangled ahead of the boat, in the direction of travel. Fish entering the current flow are stunned and retrieved with dip nets.

Electrofishing can be done from the bank as well. The process is described in "Survival Poaching" by Ragnar Benson. A portable generator is set up and one end of one line is connected to one side of the 110 receptacle socket. The other end is attached to the tip of an insulated pole. Another line is then inserted into the remaining side of the 110 receptacle and it's other end is placed in the water of a small pond. The generator is started up and the pole is moved through the water. Fish caught between the pole and the loose end of wire in the water will be stunned. The fish are then collected. Of course, retrieving the fish cannot be done until the generator is shutoff.

A couple of caveats here: we are talking about currents high enough to injure and kill an individual. Done properly, by trained individuals who are protected by rubber boots, rubber gloves and established procedures, this is a safe process. **I don't advocate** this method of fishing. If you are going to try this, or think that you may someday want to try it, do some online research. Try a Google search for "accidental deaths due to electrocution during amateur electrofishing."

Then do a search for "electrofishing procedures" to find recognized safe methods of carrying this out. You will be able to download manuals on the method

That wraps up the easiest ways to harvest fish that I have been able to find. There are no doubt others. I am continuing to do research into early methods of fish harvesting, in particular aboriginal methods from around the world and from developing countries. In early times and currently, in nations not as economically well off as most of those in the West, fishing is a serious business. Individual and family survival has depended on catching fish in the most economical and easiest ways possible. That is exactly the kind of information that I am looking for with my research into survival fishing.

Whatever I find will be incorporated into future editions of this book. If you have purchased this copy and wish to be informed of future updates, send your email address to me at the contact info on the last page, and I will send you a PDF of the my next edition.

11 PREPARING AND PRESERVING FISH

CLEANING AND COOKING

Fish spoils quickly after death, especially on a hot day. Prepare fish for eating as soon as possible after catching it.

For immediate consumption, cut out the gills and large blood vessels that lie near the spine. Gut a fish that is more than 10 centimeters (4 inches) long. If you are going to grill your catch, then scale or skin the fish, if it has large scales. If the scales are small and your catch is easily scaled, leave the skin on so you get the benefit of the fat.

 You can impale a whole small fish (less than 10 cm or 4") on a stick and cook it over an open fire. However, boiling the fish with the skin on is the best way to get the most food value. The fats and oil are under the skin and, by boiling, you can save the juices for broth.

You can use any of the methods used to cook plant food to cook fish. Fish is done when the meat flakes off. If you plan to keep the fish for later, smoke and dry it.

PRESERVATION PROCESSES

Fresh fish rapidly deteriorate unless some way can be found to preserve it. Traditionally the five ways of preserving fish have been drying, salting, pickling, canning and freezing.

Today we have access to numerous refrigerators, freezers, dehydrators, smokers, canners and other equipment to preserve our food. The individual types of equipment are similar to one another within their category. I am not going to discuss contemporary techniques of preservation because the information is prevalent on the internet, in manufacturer's equipment or user manuals, even in books in your nearest bookstore or library. Check the Resources page for canning references.

I am going to focus on methods that have been used in earlier times or are even now being used in developing nations. These low tech methods have thousands of years of trial and error behind them. Over the last four decades, aid groups have examined them and made technically appropriate suggestions and revisions to improve them further. If individuals using minimal resources and very little money can put these methods to effective use, I am sure that you can as well, whatever your situation.

If you are faced with a survival situation in the wilderness, or a social upheaval of massive proportions, you can use the methods described in this book to catch large quantities of fish, and then preserve your catch from spoilage.

The oldest traditional way of preserving fish was to let it dry by exposing it to the wind and the sun. Dried fish can have a storage life of up to a year. Most bacteria, yeasts and molds need the water in food to grow, and drying effectively prevents them from surviving in the food or spoiling it after drying.

The method is cheap and effective in suitable climates; the work can be done locally by the fisherman and family, and the resulting product is easily transported since much of the water weight is removed. Having said that, proper storage of the dried fish is critical to how long it lasts. If the climate or storage location is humid, the dried fish will absorb moisture and at some point it will become a hospitable environment for bacteria, mold, and other pests. That is where salting comes in.

Salting requires a store of salt. What is now thought to have been the first city in Europe is Solnitsata, in Bulgaria, which was a salt mine. It has provided the area now known as the Balkans with salt since 5400 BC. Even the name Solnitsata means "salt works".

There are written mentions of the Egyptians using salt in meat processing 5,000 years ago.

fig. 60

Ancient peoples, in the old world and the new, learned how to extract salt from sea water through evaporation. Sea water was directed to basins dug near the shore and allowed to evaporate in the sun. Salt springs hundreds or thousands of miles inland were used for the same purpose.

Salt has also been extracted from inland salt lakes. Sometimes salt deposits are found, leftover from prehistoric seas that have dried up, and salt can be simply mined.

Salted fish will keep for an extended period of time. The combination of salting and air drying will create a food product that you can safely store for over a year. While I could not find specific dates, probably because storage times can be affected by how you salted and dried your catch and how much humidity there is in your storage location, we know that long sea voyages were taken by explorers and merchants hundreds of years ago and that salt fish packed in barrels was a staple of the sailors diets.

Freezing was not much of an option before artificial refrigeration, at least in temperate climates, though ice houses/wells were a common way of extending the "best before date" of food. Refrigeration as a method of preserving food dates back to at least the ancient Roman and Chinese empires. Caves in which underground water freezes through the winter and then lasts well into the spring and summer were no doubt used by peoples in prehistoric times.

Refrigeration will keep fresh fish safe to eat for 3-4 days, if the storage temperature is 40^0 F. Shellfish will keep $12 - 24$ hours if fresh and twice that if cooked. Freezing extends lean fish like cod or flounder for 6 months and fatty fish like salmon two months. Modern processing methods involving freezing and vacuum packing will keep fish good for up to two years.

Before electrically powered refrigerators, people cut thick blocks of ice in the winter time and transported them to insulated warehouses where the blocks were stacked and then further covered with straw. I remember the "ice man" delivering blocks of ice to our house in St. Catharines, Ontario, when I was very young. The ice block fit into a compartment in the "ice box" and kept milk and food cool as it slowly melted. Every few days the ice man would be back with another block.

fig. 61

On my grandfather's farm in   Saskatchewan they had an "Ice house."

This was a small building with thick walls filled with sawdust that straddled a well that might have been 12 feet deep. There was a trap door in the middle of the floor that opened to reveal the well. In the wooden sill around the opening various hooks were set.

In the winter time they would cut blocks of ice (I don't know where they came from…probably a pond on the farm) and then fill the well about half full. In the warm weather, milk pails, hams, chunks of beef, and mesh bags full of whatever you wanted to keep cold would be secured to ropes, lowered into the well and then hung from the hooks near the top. I have no clue what the temperature was, but I have no doubt it was cold. This technique has been used for a long time. A cuneiform tablet from c. 1780 BC records the construction of an icehouse in the northern Mesopotamian town of Terqa (Wikipedia). That's almost 4,000 years ago.

Ice House by Maxwell Hamilton https://creativecommons.org/licenses/by/2.0/legalcode   fig. 62

Canning will extend the safe usage life of fish for years. Here is what the US Department of Agriculture says about canned goods and "Best By" dates.

- *A "Best if Used By/Before" indicates when a product will be of best flavor or quality. It is not a purchase or safety date.*
- *A "Sell-By" date tells the store how long to display the product for sale for inventory management. It is not a safety date.*
- *A "Use-By" date is the last date recommended for the use of the product while at peak quality. It is not a safety date except for when used on infant formula.*

Safety After Date Passes

If the date passes during home storage, a product should still be safe and wholesome if handled properly until the time spoilage is evident. Spoiled foods will develop an off odor, flavor or texture due to naturally occurring spoilage bacteria. If a food has developed such spoilage characteristics, it should not be eaten.

We know that canned food salvaged from sites over a hundred years old has been examined in research labs and found safe to eat. Quality of the food and nutritional values start to drop off after a few years, depending on the product and exact process used, but you can rest assured that, based on the US Department of Agriculture recommendations, canned fish will be good for years.

Canning and pickling both require specialized equipment and the instructions are detailed and this is not something you want to make a mistake with. The simplest thing for me to do is to point you to online resources. Here are free downloadable instructions from the US Department of Agriculture about canning, including canning fish:

http://nchfp.uga.edu/publications/publications_usda.html

Below is a great resource, the University of Minnesota Extension page for "Pickled Fish:"

http://www.extension.umn.edu/food/food-safety/preserving/meat-fish/pickled-fish/

At the bottom of the University of Minnesota page is a link to a downloadable video (MP4) on the pressure canning process.

HANDLING FISH

How you handle the fish you catch, and how quickly you can start the processing of your catch has a significant impact on the quality of your preserved catch. Fish caught in traps, small nets or a hand line are generally exposed to less trauma then fish caught with lines set out overnight, or with gill nets. Fish that suffer bruising will provide a lower quality of flesh.

If possible, keep fish fresh with a "live well." This is nothing more than a pail or container that can be set in the water and that fresh water can circulate through.

If the fish can't be kept alive until they are brought home, then they should be killed, bled and cleaned as soon as possible. Cleaned fish keep longer than dead whole fish.

If processing can't be started immediately, keep the fish in a shaded and cool container that allows circulation. A basket covered with a damp cloth (cloth or cover supported away from the fish) and shaded will help maintain the quality of your catch. Water evaporating from the cloth will provide some localized cooling. There is a reason most preserving of fish was done on location, right at the seashore, or on the river bank. Fish starts to spoil quickly, and processed fish weighs less than fresh, so transport after processing is easier.

CLEANING

Small fish (8" long and up to ¼ pound in weight) should be simply slit up the belly and have the entrails removed.

They should be washed out with clean water and then can be processed as is. Larger fish should have the heads cut off, be allowed to bleed and then have the two side fillets removed by cutting along the backbone from the head end to the tail. Remove the piece by working your way from the backbone down towards the belly. Turn the fish over and make a similar cut on the other side.

Both fillets must be rinsed with clean water. Remove all slime, specks of blood, membrane etc. and then place it on a draining rack to remove loose water.

SALTING PROCESS

Salting can be used on its own or as a step in drying and smoking. It immediately begins to draw moisture out of the fish. It doesn't matter what type of salt you have, however a mixture of fine and coarse salt will give the best finished product.

Larger fish should be filleted and fillets cut into pieces 15 cm (6") long.

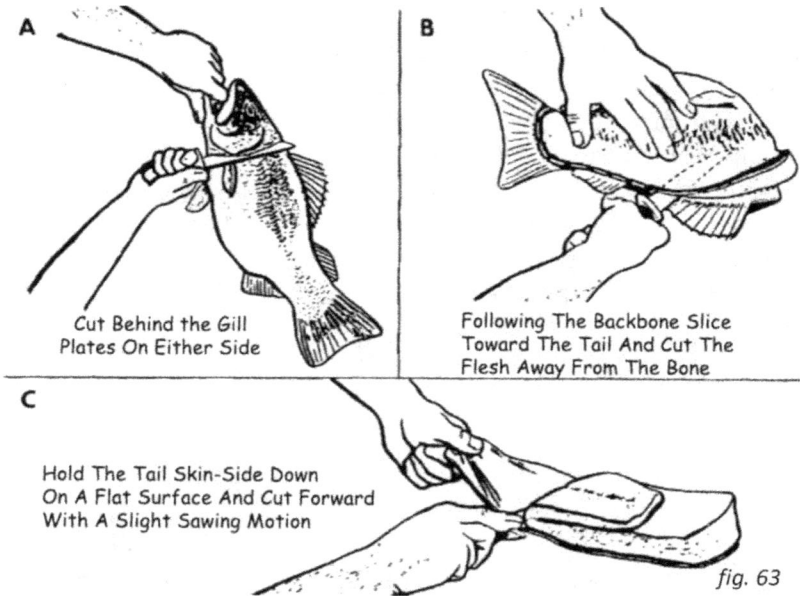

A

Cut Behind the Gill
Plates On Either Side

B

Following The Backbone Slice
Toward The Tail And Cut The
Flesh Away From The Bone

C

Hold The Tail Skin-Side Down
On A Flat Surface And Cut Forward
With A Slight Sawing Motion

fig. 63

Fill a container with salt. Remove a piece of fish from the draining rack and rub salt into it and on all sides of it, ensuring that the salt gets into any cuts, if you have made any in that piece.

Pack each piece of fish into a salting container and continue until done.

SALTING YOUR FISH

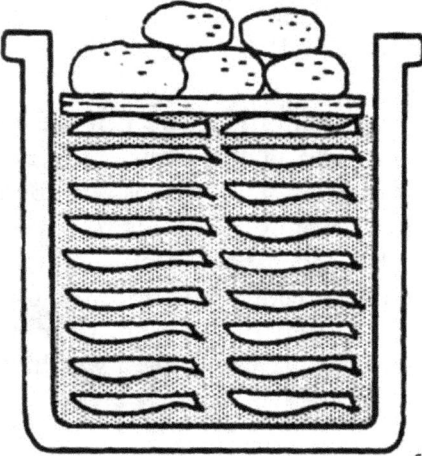

fig. 64

There are two methods of salting; dry salting and wet salting. As you might expect wet salting uses brine, which is typically about 2-3 pounds of salt to a gallon of water. Place a layer of salt on the bottom of a leak proof container, then alternate layers of fish and salt until near the top. You can place a board on top of the fish and weight it down, and then you may add water until the fish is covered.

For dry salting, use a container that will drain, such as a basket or wooden box with floorboards that have slight gaps. Use one part salt

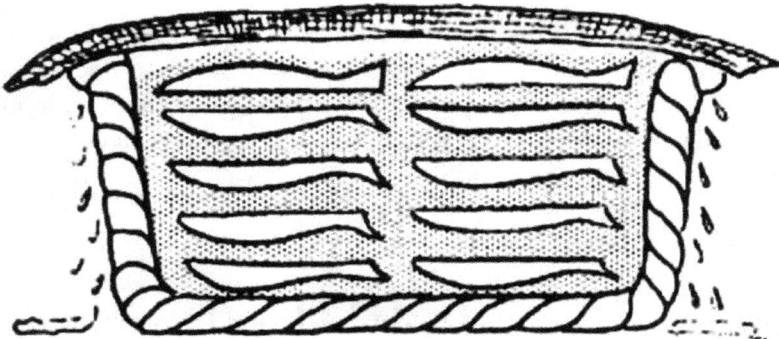

fig. 65

to three parts fish. Start with a layer of salt and then alternate fish and salt until you end with a layer of salt. The layers of salt should be about as thick as the layers of fish. Place a weighted board on top of the pile. Cover the container with a breathable covering of cloth or mesh and store in a location where the moisture can drain away.

Your containers should be raised off the ground on bricks or pieces of wood and should be in a shaded cool place.

The salting process will be more uniform if the fish are repacked every 24 hours so that their position in the stack is reversed. Fish previously on top are now on the bottom and those on the bottom are now on the top. The simplest way to do this is to have another container of the same size as the loaded one. Place a layer of salt in the bottom and just start packing it, taking fish from the top of the existing container and placing them in the bottom. Continue until you complete the process with a final layer of salt, a weighted board and breathable covering.

Fish will be ready in 5 – 10 days, depending on temperature and local humidity. Wet salted fish stored at ambient temperature should keep for two months. If kept at cooler temperatures, it will be good for upwards of three months.

DRYING AND SMOKING

Fish that have been salted will keep better if they go through a further process of drying and smoking. Smoking imparts additional flavour to the fish and is preferred by many people to simply drying, though it may limit the ways in which the fish may be served.

DRYING

Drying is generally done out of doors. A period of low humidity is required. The length of time required depends on local weather conditions.

A small fire, generating quantities of smoke will help keep flies off the fish during the first day, if flies are a problem. If the fish are on mesh racks, turn them every few hours to ensure the smoke can get to all sides.

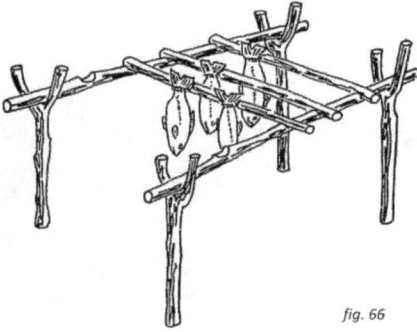

fig. 66

Fish will taste better if they are not kept under the noon day sun. They can be started in the morning sun, but should have shade at the day's peak. At night fish should be moved inside, where there is no chance of moisture from rain or dew.

Drying time will depend on the size of the fish and the conditions. Small fish might be done in three days. Larger fish or bigger pieces could take up to ten days. When you cannot make a dent in the fish flesh when squeezed between your forefinger and thumb, the fish is dry.

Once the fish are done, an additional 2-3 hour stint of drying, every two weeks, will help prolong their quality and storage time. This also gives you an opportunity to check for spoilage.

fig. 67

89

Figures 67 and 68 show two different methods of drying fish. The principal difference in these two setups is that one suits larger fish in Iceland, the other suits large quantities of smaller fish in Africa. Consider temperatures and humidity as well.

fig. 68

SMOKING FISH

Smoking is done to mainly provide additional flavour. The keeping characteristics of smoked fish depend more on the drying process than the smoking.

Fish will need to be suspended above a small fire that will be generating the low heat and smoke required. There are two different smoking techniques. Cold smoking moves the fish away from the heat of the fire. It takes longer, up to 5 – 7 days for the salted fish to take on the smoke flavour.

fig 69

Hot smoking uses a heat that can easily be felt with your hand. You should be able to keep your hand in the vicinity of the fish. If you can't the temperature is too high. What you are essentially doing is slow cooking the fish. A low smoldering fire that is maintained for 8 hours is typically required, depending on the fat content of the fish and the size of the pieces. After this initial period, 2 – 3 hours of heavy smoke are necessary to finish the fish off. Hot smoking is frequently done with barrels or old 55 gal drums. Of course, the drums must be clean of any residue and safe to use.

fig. 70

The best fuels to use are hardwood chips or sawdust. Typically these smaller forms of fuel generate more smoke than large pieces of wood. Green wood may be used as well. Soaking chips and then enclosing them in perforated metal boxes (as are used in propane barbecues) can work for small quantities.

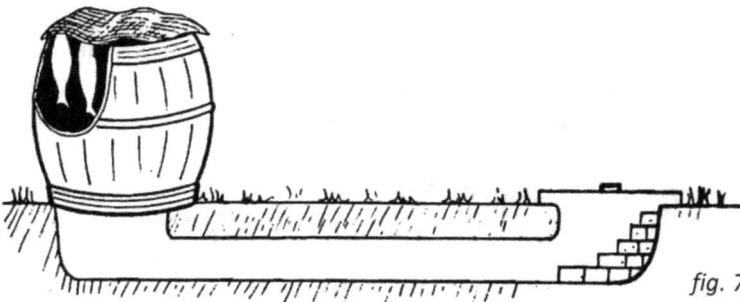

fig. 71

Smoking using barrels can be difficult because of the necessity of careful fire management to prevent flare ups and the limited amount of fish that can be processed at once.

The development of the "Chorkor oven" in Ghana in the 1970's was a vast improvement in terms of quantity of fish that could be processed, the amount of fuel used and the quality of the finished product.

fig. 72

In the image above (Figure 72) you can see the multiple trays of fish arranged over openings in the oven. This allows the simultaneous processing of large quantities of fish. The fish smoked this way are typically of a smaller variety but larger fish, cut into suitably sized pieces, could be processed as well.

The fish is first cooked over a high fire and then smoke-dried in one to five days (and nights) over a low fire. The smoking time depends on fish size and market demand in the countries where this smoker is used. Sometimes the market wants "fresh-dried" fish, while "hard-dried" fish with a longer storage life is produced for the off season and for distant markets. Fresh-dried fish keeps for up to a week, while hard-dried fish keeps for several months.

The diagrams below (Figures 73/74) provide construction details. A Chokor oven can be relatively easily produced, using concrete blocks, bricks, clay, metal plates and angle iron, or concrete.

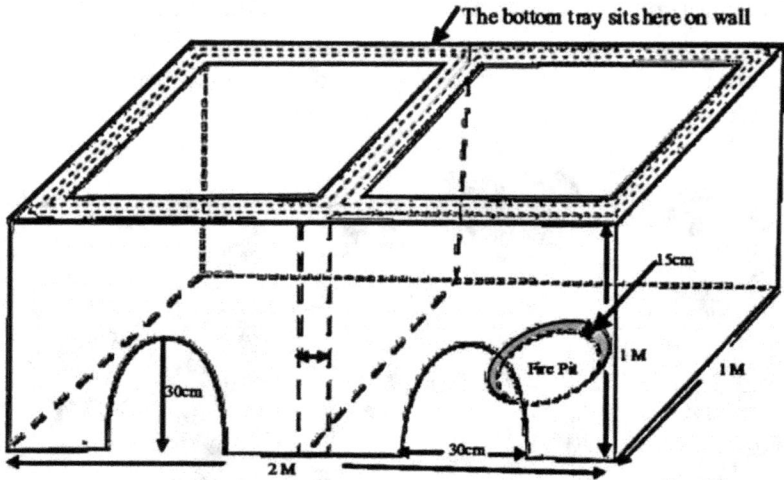

The bottom tray sits here on wall

Fire Pit

15cm

1 M

1 M

30cm

30cm

2 M

fig. 73

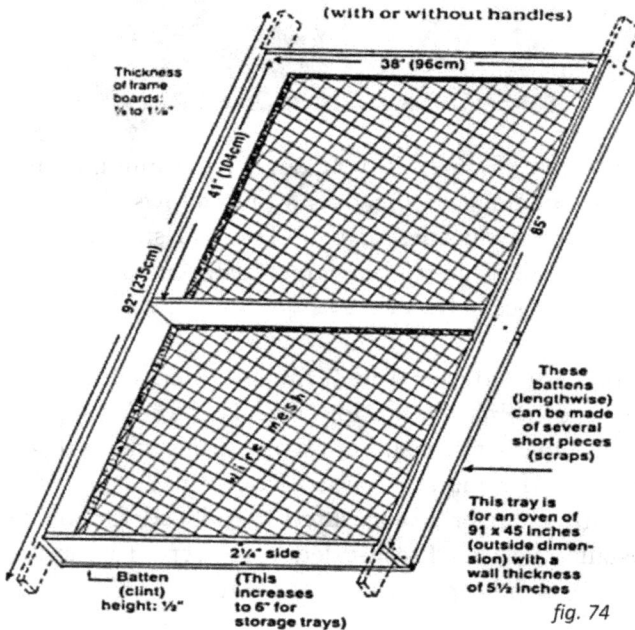

(with or without handles)

Thickness
of frame
boards:
½ to 1⅛"

38" (96cm)

41" (104cm)

92" (235cm)

85"

Wire mesh

These
battens
(lengthwise)
can be made
of several
short pieces
(scraps)

This tray is
for an oven of
91 x 45 inches
(outside dimen-
sion) with a
wall thickness
of 5½ inches

2¼" side

Batten
(clint)
height: ½"

(This
increases
to 6" for
storage trays)

fig. 74

Individual trays with wire mesh bottoms allow significant quantities of fish to be loaded above the smoke vents and the trays can be rotated if necessary to provide a consistent product. The fish being

94

smoked could also be sorted by size and the trays could be left
processing for the time required by each tray.

fig. 75

A piece of equipment like this is more than an individual would need,
but would be of value to a family group or a community. It provides
the ability to process large quantities of fish but could also be used
for different types of wild game in the production of smoke
processed jerky.

12 EATING PRESERVED FISH

In the previous pages of this book I have explained and illustrated numerous ways to ensure as steady and effective a catch of fish as is possible. As they say in the TV commercials, results may vary, but the techniques and strategies outlined have been culled from personal experience and more than 60 different military survival manuals, outdoors guides, and carefully vetted instructions from credible national and international aid and development agencies.

Fish harvesting has been approached from the perspective of what has worked in the past, what is working now and how can it be done with the lowest level of technology possible (with the possible exception of electro-fishing).

We have also covered ways that you can store your catch, putting a particular emphasis on how to handle large numbers of fish so that they can safely be stockpiled without going bad and presenting a risk to anyone consuming them.

But next comes cooking. I think it is safe to say that very few readers will have had any experience with using salted or dried fish. And for most, their exposure to pickled or smoked fish has been limited. The one area where there may be a wider exposure is probably the most technologically advanced storage method, canning. And cans of tuna or salmon are sitting in most people's pantries.

I am not going to includes recipes or instructions on how to make salmon loaf, salmon patties, salmon burgers, and salmon salad sandwiches or how to sprinkle canned salmon over a bowl of greens to make a salad. Most folks are likely to already have favourite versions of these meals and different variations are easy to find online or in your mothers recipe files.

The same can be said of tuna salad sandwiches, tuna cakes, tuna casserole, tuna melt, tuna burgers or tuna mac-n-cheese.

I might as well provide instructions for how to make a peanut butter and jelly sandwich. Dealing with salted and dried fish is a little bit more involved than grabbing a can and a can opener.

I encourage you to try some of the recipes I am going to include below before you ever need to use them. The golden rule of food storage, whether for prepping or simply as an economic measure, is to store what you eat, and eat what you store. I am not advising you to store salted, dried and/or smoked fish in this volume, but I am advising you to have purchased some at your local stores and tried various recipes before you ever need to use fish in a disaster situation, so you know what to do if the time ever comes that fish provides a significant portion of your diet.

DRIED FISH

Dried Fish Soup

This recipe has been adapted from a traditional Ghanaian one for "Dry Fish Light Soup"

½ pound dried fish cut into bite sized pieces

1 eggplant diced

2 bell peppers, diced

3 diced tomatoes (or 1 can)

1 sliced onion

okra or substitute (beans, cabbage or to taste)

powdered shrimp (or cornstarch) for thickening

2 cloves of garlic, minced

2 tsp ginger minced

1 tsp salt

additional water as required

Wash the fish twice, using fresh water each time. Put the onion, garlic and ginger into a saucepan and sauté for 3-5 minutes, until onion is tender. Add the pepper, tomatoes, and eggplant with enough water to prevent burning and cook until tender, another 5 minutes (you can skip adding water if you used canned, diced tomatoes). Add the fish and adjust the liquid content. Add okra, beans or cabbage. Cook for 20 to 25 minutes. Add additional water to reach the consistency you desire. Add thickening agent. Stir until soup thickens. Remove from heat and let stand 5 minutes.

The quantities I have used here are broad suggestions. Try making this and take notes on what you like or didn't like and adjust next time. Recipes are not hard and fast and they vary from region to region. A soup is a great way to use any dried meat, as it provides an opportunity to rehydrate the meat and increase the bulk. You could also consider using a powdered vegetable, chicken or beef broth instead of plain water.

As for vegetables, okra, beans, cabbage, all serve the function of adding texture, colour, nutrients, vitamins and minerals to the meal. Use what you have. Change things up to keep it interesting.

SALTED FISH

Salted fish need to be soaked in cold water for 8- 16 hours, with four changes of water to remove the heavy salt content. Below are a couple of different ways to use your fish.

Salted Fish Casserole

2 pounds of salted fish

5 large potatoes peeled and sliced

3 large onions sliced

¾ cups olive oil

2 cloves of garlic, minced

1 tsp red pepper flakes

I tsp paprika

3 tbsp. tomato sauce

Soak salted fish in cold water for 16 hours, as described, with at least 4 changes of water. Heat a large pot of fresh water to boiling. Add fish and cook for 5 minutes. Drain and cool. Set fish aside.

Preheat oven to 375 degrees F.

In an 8 x 11 oven proof dish layer half the potato slices, all the cod and all the onions. Cover with the rest of the potato slices. In a bowl mix together the oil, garlic, paprika, pepper flakes and tomato sauce. Poor over the potato fish mixture.

Cook in oven about 45 minutes or until done.

Fish Cakes

1 pound of salted fish

2 large potatoes, peeled and cubed

1 tsp of black pepper

½ tsp of garlic powder

2 tbsp. of dry parsley

2 beaten eggs

1 large onion chopped

½ cup of flour

3 tbsp. oil for frying

Soak salted fish in cold water for 16 hours, as described, with at least 4 changes of water. Cut into pieces about 3" in length.

Put potatoes and cod into a pot and cover with water. Bring to a boil then reduce heat to a simmer and cover. Cook for 20 minutes until potatoes are tender and cod flakes easily. Drain and cool for 20 minutes.

Mash the potato and cod pieces together roughly. Add pepper, garlic powder, and parsley. Continue mashing and stop while the mixture is still somewhat lumpy. Add the onion and beaten eggs and stir until combined. Form into balls about 1 ½" in diameter and roll in flour. Flatten slightly with hands.

Heat oil in a frying pan and cook the fish mixture about three minutes a side, until crispy and golden brown on both sides. Drain on paper towel.

Saltfish Buljol

8 ounces of salted fish

4 tbsp. of oil

2 onions chopped

3 tomatoes chopped

2 bell peppers chopped

½ tsp of pepper

1 tbsp. lemon juice

Bring the saltfish to a boil in a large pot of water. Drain and repeat. Flake the fish and press out excess water.

In a large skillet sauté the onions, tomatoes and peppers in the oil for 2 minutes. Add the flaked saltfish, pepper and lemon juice. Cook until moisture has almost all gone.

Serve with bread/toast and/or scrambled eggs.

Saltfish with Tomatoes and Olives

2 pounds salted fish

4 tbsp. lemon juice

1 pound of thickly sliced potatoes

2 large onions cut into wedges

3 tomatoes cut into wedges

2 bay leaves

2 tbsp. olive oil

¼ cups olives chopped

2 tbsp. parsley

Soak salted fish in cold water for 16 hours, as described, with at least 4 changes of water.

Sprinkle fish with lemon juice. Preheat oven to 350 degrees F. Arrange layers of fish, potatoes, onions and tomatoes in a baking dish. Arrange bay leaves on top. Drizzle with oil.

Bake until potatoes are tender and fish flakes easily. Add olives and parsley and bake for an additional 3 minutes.

13 IN CONCLUSION

I have listed more than 30 different methods of catching fish in this book. I've talked about:

1. Angling
2. Noodling
3. Trout tickling
4. Set lines
5. Trot lines
6. Drop lines
7. Limb lines
8. Jug lines
9. Stakeout lines
10. Montagnais Nightline
11. Gill nets
12. Seine nets
13. Dip nets
14. Lift nets
15. Basket fish traps
16. Pole fish traps
17. Fish weirs
18. Net fish traps
19. Stone fish traps
20. Chicken wire fish traps
21. Spearfishing
22. Bowfishing
23. Chop fishing

24. Gaff fishing
25. Snagging
26. Poison
27. Mud Stirring
28. Dynamiting
29. Shooting
30. Rock Concussion
31. Electrofishing
32. Snaring fish
33. Snaring crabs and crayfish

It bears repeating that many of these methods are illegal almost everywhere, and the legalities of others vary. It is up to you to determine the regulations that apply in your jurisdiction.

However you would want to practice these techniques before you need them if it is at all possible. Many of these methods of harvesting are legal on some species. Many of these methods are legal in modified form. Do what you can to try them out. Typically, setting up a limb line or a jug line that is tethered to shore and attended is perfectly legal. Setting up a dozen limb lines, maybe not so much. Check with local authorities or read the local fishing regulations carefully. If you do not use hooks in your bait, you should be able to safely try some of these methods out. Missing bait indicates a potential catch.

It only makes sense if you are prepping that you consider these methods in the context of your particular environment. Do you have easy access to a lake, a small pond, a stream or a river? The methods you might want to use depend on the body of water you will be harvesting from.

Once you have considered your locality and determined what strategies and techniques might make the most sense for you, make some purchases ahead of time to save yourself a lot of grief if you ever have to use any of these tactics. There is no need to create a gill net, out of paracord fibres after the SHTF, when you can buy one that is 80 feet long and 4 feet high or a prefabricated setline for the cost of lunch for two at a fast food restaurant.

Throw nets are legal for catching bait fish in many jurisdictions. That means you can practice using a throw net, catch and keep bait fish while letting any larger fish go, and get some valuable practice of your throwing technique before you ever have to consider using it for your daily meals.

If you go online and search for "DIY bait trap fishing" you will find a ton of results. Or you can do the same search on Google, but specify "video" results. It doesn't get any easier

If you have a chance to travel to vacation locations where some of these methods are legal, then take the opportunity to try them out under non-stressful conditions. Skills and techniques once learned are going to be there for you if you need to call on them in the future. Like riding a bicycle, you may get rusty, but you almost never forget how to do it.

I began this book talking about the importance of accessible protein sources for optimum functioning in an emergency or survival situation.

Fish can certainly provide you with that. I mentioned how most jurisdictions have had to create laws and rules about how and how many fish you could take because fish are not actually that difficult to catch, if you are only concerned with harvest, not sport.

In a survival situation, or if you are faced with a societal breakdown, worry about game wardens is not going to be a huge issue. And the ability to set and walk away from numerous different types of fish harvesting set ups will allow you to multiply your effectiveness, giving you time to work on other tasks that will ensure the survival of you, your family and your group.

I have provided instructions for air drying, salting and smoking your catch. I described how people kept food refrigerated and cool before modern refrigeration was invented. We discussed techniques that would allow you to process large amounts of fish at a time. And on the resource page you can find links I have provided to instructions on canning and pickling fish from highly reliable sources. I hope I was able to provide you with useful and helpful information.

I can't emphasize how important it is to try using as many of these techniques as is possible NOW, before you need them. Make it a point to try and do more fishing, even if it is simple angling. That will allow you to increase your knowledge of your local fish environment as well as learn about fish habits, local species, their preferred bait at different times of the year and the best times and conditions for fishing.

Try some of the do-it-yourself projects I have provided links to. It will only take a few hours to fabricate spear points, arrowheads, and traps. It will be time well spent even if you don't use them, because they will be there for your use if they are ever needed.

Additional time spent fishing will reward you with more quality protein, and lower grocery bills. You can put that extra money you can put towards your preparedness expenses.

You will wind up with increased skills and you will have further secured your family against a range of emergencies. Win/win.

Thanks for buying this book. If you have any comments or suggestions for improvements, I would love to hear them. Just shoot me an email at pstevens2@gmail.com

Paul Stevens

ONLINE RESOURCES

The Survival Podcast…http://www.thesurvivalpodcast.com/

Harvesting Seaweed and Shellfish…The "Conservation College" website. Specific to Washington State, but with guidelines and suggestions you can easily transfer to your locale:
www.wolfcollege.com/edible-seaweeds-and-shellfish-of0the-salish-sea

Prepare and Cook Seaweed: http://www.wikihow.com/Prepare-and-Cook-Seaweed

Harvesting Shellfish… British Columbia guidance: https://goo.gl/xg1HN0

Use the search term "harvesting shellfish (my location)" for specific guidance.

Expedient Fishing…US Army Aviation Center – Aviation Survival, Part III – Sustenance: http://www.preppers.info/uploads/us_army_cc_av0663_aviation_survival_part_iii_sustenance.pdf

Study into the use of Setlines: https://goo.gl/EOQCq1

Effectiveness of Hook Style, Bait Type and River Location on Trotline Catches: https://goo.gl/UxU5e9

Net Making instruction on YouTube: https://goo.gl/nNp4YD

How to Throw a Cast Net https://goo.gl/NxYLu4

For a look at crayfish traps, try Terry Bullard's website: http://www.terrybullard.com/CrawfishStart.html

DIY crayfish traps https://goo.gl/d24ETa

How to Make a Crab Snare: https://goo.gl/0biVXh

Fish Trapping: http://www.fao.org/3/a-x2590e/x2590e01.htm
DIY fishing bait traps: https://goo.gl/jpr892

Smoked Fish: http://seafood.oregonstate.edu/.pdf%20Links/Smoked-Fish-Virginia-Tech.pdf

http://seafood.oregonstate.edu/.pdf%20Links/Smoked-Fish-Part-II-Virginia-Tech.pdf
http://seafood.oregonstate.edu/.pdf%20Links/Smoked-Fish-Part-III-Virginia-Tech.pdf

Smoking and Canning: http://essentialstuff.org/wp-content/uploads/2011/02/Fish-preservation_JH_021310.pdf

Home Curing Fish: http://pdf.usaid.gov/pdf_docs/Pnaaf858.pdf

Chokor Ovens: http://www.crc.uri.edu/download/GH2014_ACT050_CEW_FIN508-1.pdf

SURVIVALFISHING

ABOUT THE AUTHOR

Paul Stevens was brought up in a family where respect for the outdoors and personal independence were strong values. Early life experience on the small farms of his extended family, in home vegetable gardens, and canning and freezing of family grown produce, made having a large pantry a commonplace.

A career in the nuclear industry and positions in emergency response within that field inculcated a philosophy of preparedness. Personal experience of multi-day power outages only reinforced the possibility of infrastructure breakdown. And a growing awareness of possible threats to the electrical grid from pandemic, economic breakdown, cyber-attack, solar storms and EMP attack lead to an interest in the preparedness field with regards to society and the individual family. Paul continues to research and learn in the prepping field and looks forward to assembling additional books in the near future.

Paul may be contacted at pstevens2@gmail.com

www.ingramcontent.com/pod-product-compliance
Lightning Source LLC
Chambersburg PA
CBHW050530280326
41933CB00011B/1531